GRADE
5

MATH Trailblazers®

A BALANCED MATHEMATICS PROGRAM INTEGRATING SCIENCE AND LANGUAGE ARTS

Unit Resource Guide
Unit 3

Fractions and Ratios

D0943416

THIRD EDITION

KENDALL/HUNT PUBLISHING COMPANY
4050 Westmark Drive   Dubuque, Iowa 52002

A TIMS® Curriculum
University of Illinois at Chicago

UIC The University of Illinois
at Chicago

The original edition was based on work supported by the National Science Foundation under grant No. MDR 9050226 and the University of Illinois at Chicago. Any opinions, findings, and conclusions or recommendations expressed in this publication are those of the author(s) and do not necessarily reflect the views of the granting agencies.

Letter Home

Fractions and Ratios

Date: _____

Dear Family Member:

Children first learn about fractions from listening to adult conversation: "I'll be there in a half hour," or "The recipe calls for $\frac{2}{3}$ cup of sugar." As children's experiences with fractions grow, they begin to use the language of fractions in their lives. "You can have half my sandwich," or "I need half a dollar." However, many times a child's understanding of fractions is not complete.

Children do not always realize that when something is divided into fractions, the parts must be equal. You often hear children say, "My half is bigger than your half." Or children may not realize that the wholes must be the same size when comparing fractions. "I ate half the cake" has a different meaning depending on whether the whole cake is a cupcake or a wedding cake.

In this unit, your child will build models of different fractions, investigate equivalent fractions, and compare fractions. Students also will participate in a lab where they will use ratios and graphs to estimate the walking speed of a fifth grader.

Students imagine different halves when they hear the sentence "I ate $\frac{1}{2}$ of a cake."

You can increase your child's awareness and understanding of fractions by looking for places where fractions are used outside of school. Examples might include cooking with a recipe, or examining a $\frac{1}{8}$-inch drill bit from a hardware store or $2\frac{3}{8}$ yards of fabric from the fabric store.

In this unit, your child will also review the multiplication and division facts for the 2s and 3s. Use the *Triangle Flash Cards* to help your child with these facts.

Sincerely,

_____

Carta al hogar

Fracciones y razones

Fecha: _____

Estimado miembro de familia:

Los niños pequeños aprenden sobre fracciones cuando escuchan las conversaciones de los adultos: "Llegaré en media hora," "La receta lleva $\frac{2}{3}$ de taza de azúcar".

A medida que los niños tienen más experiencias con fracciones, empiezan a usar el lenguaje de las fracciones en sus vidas: "Puedes comer la mitad de mi sándwich" o "Necesito medio dólar". Sin embargo, muchas veces los niños no comprenden completamente el concepto de fracciones.

Los niños no siempre reconocen que cuando algo se divide en fracciones, las partes deben ser iguales. Muchas veces oirá que los niños dicen "Mi mitad es más grande que tu mitad". O a menudo los niños no se dan cuenta de que los objetos enteros deben ser iguales cuando se habla de fracciones. "Me comí la mitad del pastel" tiene un significado diferente si se trata de un pastelito individual o un pastel de boda.

Los estudiantes imaginan diferentes mitades cuando escuchan la oración "Me comí $\frac{1}{2}$ del pastel".

En esta unidad, su hijo/a construirá modelos de diferentes fracciones, investigará fracciones equivalentes, y comparará fracciones. Los estudiantes también participarán en un laboratorio experimental donde usarán razones y gráficas para estimar a qué velocidad camina un niño de quinto grado.

Usted puede ayudar a su hijo/a a reconocer y entender las fracciones buscando situaciones en las que se usan fracciones fuera de la escuela. Los ejemplos pueden incluir cocinar siguiendo una receta, mirar un taladro de $\frac{1}{8}$ de pulgada en una ferretería o comprar 2 yardas y $\frac{3}{8}$ de tela en una tienda de telas.

En esta unidad, su hijo/a también repasará las tablas de multiplicación y división por dos y tres. Use las *tarjetas triangulares* para ayudar a su hijo/a con estas tablas.

Atentamente,

_____

Table of Contents

Unit 3
Fractions and Ratios

Unit 3

Outline
Fractions and Ratios

Unit Summary

Estimated Class Sessions 11-16

Students build a strong conceptual foundation for work with fractions, ratios, and proportions. They review fraction concepts with pattern blocks and use the concepts to develop skills and procedures such as finding equivalent fractions, ordering fractions, writing mixed numbers for improper fractions, and writing improper fractions for mixed numbers.

Students explore ratios using data tables, graphs, and symbols. In the lab *Distance vs. Time,* speed is defined as the ratio of distance moved to time taken. Students use this definition as they apply their knowledge of fractions and ratios. The Student Rubric: *Knowing* is reintroduced. The DPP for this unit reviews the multiplication and division facts for the twos and threes.

Major Concept Focus

- ratios
- improper fractions
- mixed numbers
- TIMS Laboratory Method
- Student Rubric: *Knowing*
- comparing fractions
- modeling fractions with pattern blocks
- ordering fractions
- writing number sentences using fractions
- equivalent fractions
- measuring time with a stopwatch
- measuring length in yards
- point graphs
- best-fit lines
- using data to solve problems
- speed
- multiplication and division facts: 2s and 3s

Pacing Suggestions

This unit begins work with fractions and ratios. The units that follow use the fraction concepts developed in this unit to build additional skills and concepts with fractions, ratios, decimals, and proportional reasoning. These skills and concepts are developed in a careful sequence as shown below.

Unit 4: Application of ratios and proportional reasoning (Lesson 6)
Unit 5: Equivalent fractions, mixed numbers, improper fractions, ordering fractions, addition and subtraction of fractions, application of ratios and proportional reasoning
Unit 7: Decimals, percents, and probability
Unit 8: Application and assessment of fractions, decimals, and percents (Lessons 5 and 6)
Unit 9: Fractions and division, remainders as fractions
Unit 11: Fractions in lowest terms, common denominators, comparing fractions, addition and subtraction of fractions
Unit 12: Addition, subtraction, and multiplication of fractions, addition of mixed numbers, applications of fractions
Unit 13: Ratios and proportions
Unit 14: Application of ratios and proportional reasoning (Lesson 2)
Unit 16: Application and assessment of ratios and proportional reasoning (Lessons 2, 3, and 4)

- Teach the units in the order they were written. Students will revisit important concepts and skills as they experience them in new contexts as the units progress. Units that do not contain significant content on fractions and ratios will include practice and review in the Daily Practice and Problems and the Home Practice in the *Discovery Assignment Book.*

- Use the recommended session numbers for each lesson as a guide. It is not necessary to wait until students master each concept and skill as they will revisit them in later units and practice them in the Daily Practice and Problems and Home Practice throughout the year. Use the Assessment Indicators as a guide for the appropriate time to assess specific skills. The Assessment Indicators for all units are listed on the *Individual Assessment Record Sheet* which is in the Assessment section of the *Teacher Implementation Guide.*

- Unit 3 Lesson 1 *Wholes and Parts* contains a review of pattern block fractions taken from fourth-grade materials. This review is for students who have not had *Math Trailblazers* in previous years. These blackline masters are at the end of the Lesson Guide. If you use this review, students will need 2 days to complete the lesson.

- Unit 3 Lesson 7 *Speedy Problems* is an optional lesson. It is a series of word problems that are appropriate to assign for homework. The lesson is suitable for a substitute teacher since the preparation is minimal.

Assessment Indicators

Use the following Assessment Indicators and the *Observational Assessment Record* that follows the Background section in this unit to assess students on key ideas.

A1. Can students represent fractions using pattern blocks and number lines?

A2. Can students find equivalent fractions?

A3. Can students name fractions greater than one as mixed numbers or improper fractions?

A4. Can students compare and order fractions?

A5. Can students collect, organize, graph, and analyze data?

A6. Can students draw and interpret best-fit lines?

A7. Can students use ratios to solve problems?

A8. Can students measure length in yards?

A9. Do students demonstrate fluency with the multiplication and division facts for the 2s and 3s?

Unit Planner

KEY: SG = Student Guide, DAB = Discovery Assignment Book, AB = Adventure Book, URG = Unit Resource Guide, DPP = Daily Practice and Problems, HP = Home Practice (found in Discovery Assignment Book), and TIG = Teacher Implementation Guide.

	Lesson Information	Supplies	Copies/Transparencies
Lesson 1 **Wholes and Parts** URG Pages 31–50 SG Pages 68–72 DAB Pages 35–38 DPP A–B HP Parts 1–2 *Estimated Class Sessions* **1-2**	**Activity** Students use pattern blocks to model fractions, to review the concept of a whole, and to write fractions. **Math Facts** Review the multiplication and division facts for the 2s and 3s. Complete DPP item B. **Homework** 1. Assign the *Homework: Wholes and Parts* Activity Pages found in the *Discovery Assignment Book.* 2. Assign Parts 1 and 2 of the Home Practice. **Assessment** Use the homework pages in the *Discovery Assignment Book* to assess students' abilities to represent a fraction given a whole.	• 1 set of pattern blocks (2–3 yellow hexagons, 6 red trapezoids, 10 blue rhombuses, 10 green triangles, 6 brown trapezoids, 12 purple triangles) per student pair • overhead pattern blocks, optional	• 1 copy of *Introducing Pattern Block Fractions* URG Pages 40–42 per student, optional • 1 transparency of *Pattern Block Record Sheet* DAB Page 35
Lesson 2 **Fraction Sentences** URG Pages 51–62 SG Pages 73–76 DPP C–D HP Part 4 *Estimated Class Sessions* **1-2**	**Activity** Using pattern blocks, students write number sentences for a whole divided into parts. They also write number sentences that equate mixed numbers with improper fractions. **Math Facts** Review the multiplication and division facts for the 2s and 3s. Complete DPP items C and D. **Homework** 1. Assign the Homework section in the *Student Guide.* 2. Assign Part 4 of the Home Practice.	• 1 set of pattern blocks (2–3 yellow hexagons, 6 red trapezoids, 10 blue rhombuses, 10 green triangles, 6 brown trapezoids, 12 purple triangles) per student pair • overhead pattern blocks, optional	• 1 copy of *Pattern Block Record Sheet* DAB Page 35 per student, optional
Lesson 3 **Equivalent Fractions** URG Pages 63–74 SG Pages 77–81 DAB Page 39 DPP E–H *Estimated Class Sessions* **2-3**	**Activity** Students investigate equivalent fractions using pattern blocks and number lines. They write equivalent fractions for a given number. **Math Facts** Review the multiplication and division facts for the 2s and 3s. Complete DPP item E. **Homework** Assign the homework in the *Student Guide.* **Assessment** 1. Choose questions in the Homework section as assessment. 2. Use the journal prompt as an assessment.	• 1 set of pattern blocks (2–3 yellow hexagons, 6 red trapezoids, 10 blue rhombuses, 10 green triangles, 6 brown trapezoids, 12 purple triangles) per student pair • 1 ruler per student • colored chalk, optional • overhead pattern blocks, optional	• 1 transparency of *Number Lines for Fractohoppers* DAB Page 39, optional

	Lesson Information	**Supplies**	**Copies/ Transparencies**
Lesson 4 **Comparing Fractions** URG Pages 75–84 SG Pages 82–84 DPP I–J HP Parts 3 & 6 *Estimated Class Sessions* **1**	**Activity** Students compare fractions using 0, $\frac{1}{2}$, and 1 as benchmarks. They also compare fractions with like numerators or like denominators. **Math Facts** Review the multiplication and division facts for the 2s and 3s. Complete DPP item I. **Homework** 1. Assign Homework *Questions 1–6* in the *Student Guide.* 2. Assign Part 3 of the Home Practice. **Assessment** Use Part 6 of the Home Practice as an assessment.	• pattern blocks, optional	• 1 transparency of *Number Lines for Fractohoppers* chart SG Page 82
Lesson 5 **Using Ratios** URG Pages 85–109 SG Pages 85–93 DPP K–N HP Part 5 *Estimated Class Sessions* **2-3**	**Activity** Students use ratios to find the cost of items at a school fun fair. They express the ratios in words, tables, graphs, and symbols. **Math Facts** Review the multiplication and division facts for the 2s and 3s. Complete DPP item K. **Homework** 1. Assign the homework at the end of the lesson. Students will need enough graph paper to make three or four graphs. 2. Assign Part 5 of the Home Practice. **Assessment** 1. Use *Question 1* in the Homework section of the *Student Guide.* 2. Use the *Quiz Time* Assessment Pages.	• 1 ruler per student	• 1 copy of *Quiz Time* URG Pages 94–96 per student • 5 copies of *Centimeter Graph Paper* URG Page 100 per student • 1 copy of *Half-Centimeter Grid Paper* URG Page 101 per student, optional • 1 transparency of *Cost of Muffins Data Table* URG Page 97 • 1 transparency of *Cost of Muffins Graph* URG Page 98 • 1 transparency of *Using Ratios to Convert Feet to Yards* URG Page 99
Lesson 6 **Distance vs. Time** URG Pages 110–139 SG Pages 94–98 DPP O–V *Estimated Class Sessions* **4**	**Lab** Students use ratios to investigate the walking speed of a fifth grader. They review measurement, graphing, and data collection skills. **Math Facts** Review the multiplication and division facts for the 2s and 3s. Complete DPP item O. **Homework** 1. Assign the Homework section in the *Student Guide.* 2. Assign the problems in Lesson 7 *Speedy Problems.* **Assessment** 1. Use DPP item U to assess students' fluency with the multiplication and division facts for the 2s and 3s. 2. Use the *Observational Assessment Record* and the *Individual Assessment Record Sheet* as you observe students measuring length. 3. Assess students' graphing abilities by scoring their graphs.	• 3 stopwatches per student group • 1–2 metersticks per student group • chalk or tape • 1 calculator per student	• 1 copy of *Using Best-Fit Lines* URG Pages 126–131 per student, optional • 1 copy of *Centimeter Graph Paper* URG Page 100 per student • 1 copy of *Three-trial Data Table* URG Page 132 per student • 1 transparency of *Nila's Sit-Ups* URG Page 124, optional • 1 transparency of *What's Wrong with This Graph?* URG Page 125, optional • 1 transparency of *Centimeter Graph Paper* URG Page 100, optional • 1 transparency or wall chart of Student Rubric: *Knowing* TIG, Assessment section

(Continued)

	Lesson Information	Supplies	Copies/ Transparencies
	4. Use the rubrics *Knowing* and *Telling* to assess students' work on **Questions 16–18** in the Explore section. 5. Use DPP item V to assess ratio concepts.		• 1 transparency or wall chart of Student Rubric: *Telling* TIG, Assessment section • 1 copy of *TIMS Multidimensional Rubric* TIG, Assessment section • 1 copy of *Observational Assessment Record* URG Pages 11–12 to be used throughout this unit • 1 copy of *Individual Assessment Record Sheet* TIG Assessment section per student, previously copied for use throughout the year
Lesson 7 **Speedy Problems** URG Pages 140–143 SG Page 99 *Estimated Class Sessions* **1**	OPTIONAL LESSON **Optional Activity** Students solve a variety of multistep word problems. **Homework** Assign some or all of the problems for homework. **Assessment** Assess students' work on **Question 6.**	• 1 calculator per student	

Preparing for Upcoming Lessons

In Lesson 6, students use stopwatches. You may want to place stopwatches in a learning center so students become familiar with their use before this activity.

Connections

A current list of literature and software connections is available at *www.mathtrailblazers.com*. You can also find information on connections in the *Teacher Implementation Guide* Literature List and Software List sections.

Literature Connections

Suggested Titles

- Coffland, Jack. *Football Math: Touchdown Activities and Projects for Grades 4–8*. Good Year Books, Tucson, AZ, 1995.
- Jennison, Christopher. *Baseball Math: Grandslam Activities and Projects*. Good Year Books, Parsipanny, NJ, 2001.
- Schwartz, David M. *If You Hopped Like a Frog*. Scholastic Press, New York, 1999.
- Xiong, Blip. *Nine in One, Grr! Grr!* Children's Book Press, San Francisco, 1989. (Lesson 5)

Software Connections

- *Fraction Attraction* develops understanding of fractions using fraction bars, pie charts, hundreds blocks, and other materials.
- *Graph Master* allows students to collect data and create their own graphs.
- *Math Arena* is a collection of math activities that reinforces many math concepts.
- *Math Munchers Deluxe* provides practice in basic facts and finding equivalent fractions, decimals, percents, ratios, angles and identifying geometric shapes, factors, and multiples in an arcade-like game.
- *Mighty Math Number Heroes* poses short answer questions about fractions, number operations, polygons, and probability.
- *National Library of Virtual Manipulatives* website (http://matti.usu.edu) allows students to work with manipulatives including geoboards, base-ten pieces, the abacus, and many others.
- *TinkerPlots* allows students to record, compare, and analyze data in tables and graphs.

Teaching All Math Trailblazers Students

Math Trailblazers® lessons are designed for students with a wide range of abilities. The lessons are flexible and do not require significant adaptation for diverse learning styles or academic levels. However, when needed, lessons can be tailored to allow students to engage their abilities to the greatest extent possible while building knowledge and skills.

To assist you in meeting the needs of all students in your classroom, this section contains information about some of the features in the curriculum that allow all students access to mathematics. For additional information, see the Teaching the *Math Trailblazers* Student: Meeting Individual Needs section in the *Teacher Implementation Guide.*

Differentiation Opportunities in this Unit

Laboratory Experiments

Laboratory experiments enable students to solve problems using a variety of representations including pictures, tables, graphs, and symbols. Teachers can assign or adapt parts of the analysis according to the student's ability. The following lesson is a lab:

- Lesson 6 *Distance vs. Time*

Journal Prompts

Journal prompts provide opportunities for students to explain and reflect on mathematical problems. They can help both students who need practice explaining their ideas and students who benefit from answering higher order questions. Students with various learning styles can express themselves using pictures, words, and sentences. Teachers can alter journal prompts to suit students' ability levels. The following lessons contain a journal prompt:

- Lesson 1 *Wholes and Parts*
- Lesson 3 *Equivalent Fractions*

- Lesson 5 *Using Ratios*
- Lesson 6 *Distance vs. Time*

DPP Challenges

DPP Challenges are items from the Daily Practice and Problems that usually take more than fifteen minutes to complete. These problems are more thought-provoking and can be used to stretch students' problem-solving skills. The following lesson has a DPP Challenge in it:

- DPP Challenge D from Lesson 2 *Fraction Sentences*

Extensions

Use extensions to enrich lessons. Many extensions provide opportunities to further involve or challenge students of all abilities. Take a moment to review the extensions prior to beginning this unit. Some extensions may require additional preparation and planning. The following lesson contains an extension:

- Lesson 5 *Using Ratios*

Background
Fractions and Ratios

Throughout *Math Trailblazers,* students have explored and used fractions in many contexts using a variety of manipulatives. In this unit, students continue to build a strong conceptual foundation for work with fractions and ratios. They review fraction concepts and develop skills and procedures such as finding equivalent fractions, ordering fractions, writing mixed numbers for improper fractions, and writing improper fractions for mixed numbers. Students also explore ratios using data tables, graphs, and symbols. In later units, students will use the skills and concepts learned in this unit to develop meaningful procedures for adding, subtracting, and multiplying fractions. The work with ratios provides the basis for work with proportions. And, their study of fractions and ratios will connect to decimals and percents.

Types of Fractions

We encounter most fractions in the following contexts:

- part-whole fractions
- indicated divisions
- ratios
- measurements
- the names of points on a number line
- pure numbers
- probabilities

A source of confusion for students is the use of the same symbols for all these kinds of fractions. For example, the symbol "$\frac{1}{2}$" can represent a part of an object (one-half of a pizza), a part of a collection (one-half of a class), a part of a unit of measurement (one-half inch), a ratio (one part milk to two parts flour), a probability (the chance of a fair coin showing heads), a part of a distance (one-half the way to Paducah), a pure number (the average of 0 and 1), or a division (1 divided by 2).

Students need to understand that although fractions occur in different situations, the mathematical procedures for naming, comparing, and operating on fractions are the same. To make connections among the various contexts, students explore fractions and ratios using a broad selection of concrete materials and solve problems in a variety of real-life settings. In this unit, students use a part-whole model (pattern blocks) to review concepts developed in previous grades. They also investigate mixed numbers and improper fractions. And, they use a number line model to compare fractions and to find equivalent fractions. They use fractions to represent ratios such as $\frac{25¢}{2 \text{ cookies}}$ and $\frac{3 \text{ ft}}{1 \text{ yd}}$. In the lab *Distance vs. Time,* students measure the walking speed of a fifth grader ($\frac{15 \text{ yds}}{10 \text{ sec}}$) and use the data to make connections between fractions, ratios, and line graphs.

Teaching Fractions Using Manipulatives and Labs

Children need exposure to a variety of concrete models and mathematical interpretations of fractions and ratios to understand the underlying concepts before they can develop meaningful procedures with symbols (Behr and Post, 1992). Therefore, in this unit and succeeding units, students develop concepts and procedures by using manipulatives and drawings and by applying the concepts and skills in labs and real-life situations. Research in the teaching and learning of rational numbers also suggests that although students are able to draw on their informal or "real-life" knowledge of fractions to solve problems, rote procedures can interfere with attempts to construct meaningful algorithms (Mack, 1990). For example, when students are presented with a problem such as $4 - \frac{7}{8}$, their answers are often incorrect because they try to apply rote procedures which are not meaningful to them. The same students are often able to solve the problem when it is presented in a context, such as, you have four cookies and you eat $\frac{7}{8}$ of a cookie. How many cookies are left? They can use their knowledge of the real world to think through the problem and find a solution that makes sense to them.

Sequence of Concepts and Skills

This unit and those that follow include a carefully developed sequence of experiences. Students use fractions, decimals, ratios, and percents in varied contexts so they generalize concepts and procedures as they apply them to new situations. For example, they will continue their study of speed by using ratios and lines to compare speeds (Unit 5); use pattern blocks and drawings to develop procedures for operations with fractions (Units 5 and 12); explore the connections between fractions, decimals, and percents as part of the study of probability (Unit 7); use decimals to measure time and length (Units 8 and 14); and use ratios to define density and derive the formula for finding the circumference of a circle (Units 8 and 14). See the Pacing Suggestions in the Unit Outline for this unit for more information. See also the Unit Summaries and Scope and Sequence in the *Teacher Implementation Guide*.

Resources

- Behr, M.J., and T.R. Post. "Teaching Rational Number and Decimal Concepts." In *Teaching Mathematics in Grades K–8: Research Based Methods*. Allyn and Bacon, Boston, 1992.

- Caldwell, J.H. "Communicating about Fractions with Pattern Blocks." In *Teaching Children Mathematics*. Volume 2 Number 3, National Council of Teachers of Mathematics, Reston, VA, November 1995.

- Cramer, K., and T.R. Post. "Making Connections: A Case for Proportionality." In *Arithmetic Teacher*. Volume 40, Number 6, National Council of Teachers of Mathematics. Reston, VA, February 1993.

- Curcio, F.R., and N.S. Bezuk. *Understanding Rational Numbers and Proportions*. National Council of Teachers of Mathematics, Reston, VA, 1994.

- *Principles and Standards for School Mathematics*. National Council of Teachers of Mathematics, Reston, VA, 2000.

- Mack, N.K. "Learning Fractions with Understanding: Building on Informal Knowledge." In *Journal for Research in Mathematics Education*. Volume 21, Number 1, National Council of Teachers of Mathematics, Reston, VA, January 1990.

- Post, T.R., et al. "Order and Equivalence of Rational Numbers: A Cognitive Analysis." In *Journal for Research in Mathematics Education*. Volume 16, Number 1, National Council of Teachers of Mathematics, Reston, VA, January 1990.

Observational Assessment Record

A1   Can students represent fractions using pattern blocks and number lines?

A2   Can students find equivalent fractions?

A3   Can students name fractions greater than one as mixed numbers or improper fractions?

A4   Can students compare and order fractions?

A5   Can students collect, organize, graph, and analyze data?

A6   Can students draw and interpret best-fit lines?

A7   Can students use ratios to solve problems?

A8   Can students measure length in yards?

A9   Do students demonstrate fluency with the multiplication and division facts for the 2s and 3s?

A10 _____

Name	A1	A2	A3	A4	A5	A6	A7	A8	A9	A10	Comments
1.											
2.											
3.											
4.											
5.											
6.											
7.											
8.											
9.											
10.											
11.											
12.											

Name	A1	A2	A3	A4	A5	A6	A7	A8	A9	A10	Comments
13.											
14.											
15.											
16.											
17.											
18.											
19.											
20.											
21.											
22.											
23.											
24.											
25.											
26.											
27.											
28.											
29.											
30.											
31.											
32.											

Unit 3

Daily Practice and Problems
Fractions and Ratios

A DPP Menu for Unit 3

Two Daily Practice and Problems (DPP) items are included for each class session listed in the Unit Outline. A scope and sequence chart for the DPP is in the *Teacher Implementation Guide*.

Icons in the Teacher Notes column designate the subject matter of each DPP item. The first item in each class session is always a Bit and the second is either a Task or Challenge. Each item falls into one or more of the categories listed below. A menu of the DPP items for Unit 3 follows.

Ⓝ **Number Sense** A, C, D, F–J, L–N, Q, R, V	▧ **Computation** C, G, L, P, T, V	🕐 **Time** J, P, T	⬡ **Geometry**
⁵ₓ⁷ **Math Facts** B–E, I, K, O, U	$ **Money**	⬛ **Measurement** R, S	▱ **Data** F

Refer to the *Daily Practice and Problems and Home Practice Guide* in the *Teacher Implementation Guide* for further information on the DPP. The *Daily Practice and Problems and Home Practice Guide* includes information on how and when to use the DPP.

Review and Assessment of Math Facts

By the end of fifth grade, students in *Math Trailblazers* are expected to demonstrate fluency with all the facts. The DPP for this unit continues the systematic, strategies-based approach to reviewing the multiplication and division facts. This unit reviews the second group of facts, the 2s and 3s. The *Triangle Flash Cards* for the 2s and 3s follow the Home Practice for this unit in the *Discovery*

Assignment Book. Blackline masters of all the flash cards, organized by group, are in the *Grade 5 Facts Resource Guide.*

The following describes how the facts for the 2s and 3s will be practiced and assessed in the DPP for this unit.

1. DPP item B instructs students to quiz each other on the multiplication and division facts for the 2s and 3s using the *Triangle Flash Cards.* Students sort the cards into three piles: those facts they know and can answer quickly, those they can figure out with a strategy, and those they need to learn. The DPP item also reminds students to update their *Multiplication* and *Division Facts I Know* charts that they began in Lesson 2 of Unit 2.

2. DPP items C and D help students practice the multiplication facts for the 2s and 3s. DPP items E, K, and O use fact families to review the related division facts.

3. DPP item U assesses students on a mixture of multiplication and division facts. Students update both their *Multiplication* and *Division Facts I Know* charts.

Note: Part 1 of the Home Practice in the *Discovery Assignment Book* reminds students to take home their flash cards to practice the facts with a family member.

For more information about the distribution and assessment of the math facts, see the TIMS Tutor: *Math Facts* in the *Teacher Implementation Guide*. Also refer to the *Grade 5 Facts Resource Guide*.

Unit 3 · Daily Practice and Problems

Students may solve the items individually, in groups, or as a class. The items may also be assigned for homework. The DPPs are also available on the Teacher Resource CD.

Student Questions	Teacher Notes
(A) Number Changes Always begin with the number: 5,987,654,321 Change it to: A. 12 million more B. 50 thousand less C. 7 hundred more D. 200 million more E. 3 billion less	**TIMS Bit** [N] A. 5,999,654,321 B. 5,987,604,321 C. 5,987,655,021 D. 6,187,654,321 E. 2,987,654,321

Multiplication and Division Facts:
2s and 3s

With a partner, use your *Triangle Flash Cards* to quiz each other on the multiplication and division facts for the 2s and 3s. Follow the directions in the *Student Guide* for Unit 2 Lesson 2 *Facts I Know.*

As your partner quizzes you on the multiplication facts, separate the facts into three piles: those facts you know and can answer quickly, those you can figure out with a strategy, and those you need to learn. Practice any facts for the 2s and 3s that are in the last two piles. List these facts so you can practice them at home. Repeat the process for the division facts.

Circle all the facts you know and can answer quickly on your *Multiplication* and *Division Facts I Know* charts.

TIMS Task

The *Triangle Flash Cards: 2s* are in the *Discovery Assignment Book* following the Home Practice. Blackline masters of all the flash cards, organized by group, are in the *Grade 5 Facts Resource Guide.* Part 1 of the Home Practice reminds students to take home the list of 2s and 3s they need to study as well as their flash cards.

The *Multiplication* and *Division Facts I Know* charts were distributed in Unit 2 Lesson 2. See that Lesson Guide or the *Grade 5 Facts Resource Guide* for more information.

Inform students when you will give the quiz on these facts. This quiz, which assesses students on multiplication and division facts for the 2s and 3s, appears in DPP item U.

Student Questions	**Teacher Notes**

Multiplying by 10s

A. $30 \times 20 =$ B. $80 \times 30 =$

C. $200 \times 60 =$ D. $50 \times 300 =$

E. $1000 \times 30 =$ F. $900 \times 200 =$

G. $6000 \times 300 =$ H. $20 \times 200 =$

I. $7000 \times 3 =$

TIMS Bit

A. 600   B. 2400

C. 12,000   D. 15,000

E. 30,000   F. 180,000

G. 1,800,000   H. 4000

I. 21,000

D Bikes and Trikes

There are some bicycles and some tricycles in the TIMS warehouse. The total number of wheels is 35.

1. How many bikes and how many trikes might be in the TIMS warehouse? (Give several answers to this problem.)

2. What is the fewest number of bikes that can be in the warehouse? Then how many trikes will there be?

3. What is the fewest number of trikes that can be in the warehouse? Then how many bikes will there be?

4. If the warehouse has a total of 15 bikes and trikes altogether, how many of each are in the warehouse?

5. If the number of bikes and trikes is the same, how many of each are in the warehouse?

TIMS Challenge

1. Some students may get only one answer for the problem. Others may be able to make a table and exhaust the possibilities. One possible answer is: 5 trikes ($5 \times 3 =$ 15 wheels) and 10 bikes ($10 \times 2 = 20$ wheels).

2. If there is only one bike, then 35 wheels $-$ 2 wheels $=$ 33 wheels left. 33 wheels $\div$ 3 wheels each $=$ 11 trikes.

3. If there is only one trike, then 35 wheels $-$ 3 wheels $=$ 32 wheels left. 32 wheels $\div$ 2 wheels each $=$ 16 bikes.

4. 5 trikes and 10 bikes ($5 \times 3 + 10 \times 2 =$ 35 wheels)

5. 7 trikes and 7 bikes ($7 \times 3 + 7 \times 2 = 35$ wheels)

Fact Families for × and ÷

Solve each pair of related facts. Then name two other facts in the same fact family.

A. $4 \times 2 = ?$ and $8 \div 2 = ?$

B. $9 \times 3 = ?$ and $27 \div 3 = ?$

C. $3 \times 5 = ?$ and $15 \div 3 = ?$

D. $2 \times 8 = ?$ and $16 \div 8 = ?$

E. $10 \times 2 = ?$ and $20 \div 10 = ?$

F. $4 \times 3 = ?$ and $12 \div 3 = ?$

G. $7 \times 2 = ?$ and $14 \div 2 = ?$

H. $3 \times 6 = ?$ and $18 \div 3 = ?$

TIMS Bit

A. 8; 4; $2 \times 4 = 8$;
    $8 \div 4 = 2$

B. 27; 9; $3 \times 9 = 27$;
    $27 \div 9 = 3$

C. 15; 5; $5 \times 3 = 15$;
    $15 \div 5 = 3$

D. 16; 2; $8 \times 2 = 16$;
    $16 \div 2 = 8$

E. 20; 2; $2 \times 10 = 20$;
    $20 \div 2 = 10$

F. 12; 4; $3 \times 4 = 12$;
    $12 \div 4 = 3$

G. 14; 7; $2 \times 7 = 14$;
    $14 \div 7 = 2$

H. 18; 6; $6 \times 3 = 18$;
    $18 \div 6 = 3$

F Finding the Median

Use the data in the graph to answer the questions.

1. What is the most common number of pets? (What is the mode?)

2. How many students were surveyed in Room 306?

3. Use the graph to find the median number of pets owned by students in Room 306.

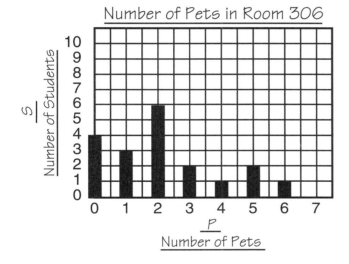

TIMS Task

1. 2 pets

2. 19 students

3. 2 pets

G Arithmetic Review

Use paper and pencil to solve these problems. Estimate to see if your answers are reasonable.

A. 54 × 8

B. 534 + 963

C. 730 × 6

D. 5001 − 3989

TIMS Bit

Do not use calculators for this review.

A. 432   B. 1497

C. 4380   D. 1012

Note that students can use a counting up strategy to solve D: 3989 + 1 = 3990; 3990 + 10 = 4000; 4000 + 1001 = 5001. So the answer is 1 + 10 + 1001 = 1012. Discuss students' strategies.

Parts of a Whole

TIMS Task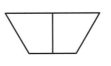

You may use pattern blocks to help you with these problems.

1. If this is $\frac{1}{2}$,

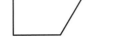

   draw 1 whole.

2. If this is one whole,

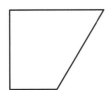

   A. Show $\frac{2}{3}$.   B. Show $\frac{4}{3}$.

1. Possible answers include:

   or

2. Possible answers include:

   A. $\frac{2}{3}$

   B. $\frac{4}{3}$

 Mixed Numbers and Improper Fractions

TIMS Bit

1. Write a whole number or a mixed number for each improper fraction.

   A. $\frac{15}{4}$ B. $\frac{24}{8}$ C. $\frac{29}{3}$

2. Write an improper fraction for each mixed number.

   A. $6\frac{2}{3}$ B. $9\frac{1}{2}$ C. $5\frac{1}{3}$

1. A. $3\frac{3}{4}$
   B. 3
   C. $9\frac{2}{3}$
2. A. $\frac{20}{3}$
   B. $\frac{19}{2}$
   C. $\frac{16}{3}$

Fraction Skip Counting

Work with a partner on these problems. Take turns timing each other.

1. Skip count by halves for 15 seconds. Write down how far you were able to count. Start like this: $\frac{1}{2}$, 1, $1\frac{1}{2}$, 2, $2\frac{1}{2}$, 3 . . .

2. Skip count by thirds for 15 seconds. Write down how far you were able to count.

3. Estimate how far you think you can count by fifths in 15 seconds. Try it. How close was your estimate?

TIMS Task

Answers will vary. To begin, you can ask the class to skip count in unison. This task provides an opportunity for students to practice starting, stopping, and resetting stopwatches. Students will use stopwatches in the lab in Lesson 6. However, they can complete this item using a clock.

K **Fact Families for × and ÷**

Complete the number sentences for the related facts.

A. $5 \times 2 =$ ___   B. $8 \times 3 =$ ___

___ $\div 5 =$ ___   ___ $\div$ ___ $= 8$

___ $\div 2 =$ ___   ___ $\div 8 =$ ___

$2 \times$ ___ $=$ ___   ___ $\times 8 =$ ___

C. $18 \div 2 =$ ___   D. $3 \times$ ___ $= 6$

___ $\times 2 =$ ___ $6 \div$ ___ $=$ ___

$18 \div$ ___ $=$ ___ $6 \div$ ___ $=$ ___

$2 \times$ ___ $=$ ___   ___ $\times 3 =$ ___

TIMS Bit

A. 10; $10 \div 5 = 2$;
   $10 \div 2 = 5$;
   $2 \times 5 = 10$

B. 24; $24 \div 3 = 8$;
   $24 \div 8 = 3$;
   $3 \times 8 = 24$

C. 9; $9 \times 2 = 18$;
   $18 \div 9 = 2$;
   $2 \times 9 = 18$

D. 2; $6 \div 2 = 3$ or
   $6 \div 3 = 2$;
   $2 \times 3 = 6$

Multiplication Practice

Solve the following problems using paper and pencil. Estimate to be sure your answers are reasonable.

A. $65 \times 27 =$ B. $58 \times 86 =$

C. $94 \times 8 =$ D. $69 \times 45 =$

E. $80 \times 46 =$ F. $937 \times 3 =$

TIMS Task

A. 1755   B. 4988

C. 752   D. 3105

E. 3680   F. 2811

M **Fractions to Order**

Arrange the fractions below in order from smallest to largest. You may use the Number Lines for Fractohoppers chart in the *Student Guide* for Lesson 4.

$\frac{5}{6}$ $\frac{1}{4}$ $\frac{1}{6}$ $\frac{2}{5}$ $\frac{1}{3}$ $\frac{3}{4}$

TIMS Bit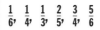

$\frac{1}{6}, \frac{1}{4}, \frac{1}{3}, \frac{2}{5}, \frac{3}{4}, \frac{5}{6}$

Pieces and Parts

Brandon says that $\frac{2}{5}$ is more than $\frac{1}{2}$ because $\frac{2}{5}$ has more pieces.

1. Is Brandon right or wrong?
2. Write a letter to Brandon explaining which is greater, $\frac{2}{5}$ or $\frac{1}{2}$, and why. Try to use a picture in your letter.

Lee Yah says that $\frac{1}{8}$ is more than $\frac{1}{6}$ because eight is more than six.

3. Is Lee Yah right or wrong?
4. Write a letter to Lee Yah explaining which is larger, $\frac{1}{6}$ or $\frac{1}{8}$, and why. Try to use a picture in your letter.

TIMS Task

1. Brandon is wrong.

2. Answers will vary; for example: If I cut one whole into 5 pieces, I will have smaller pieces than if I cut it into 4 pieces. So $\frac{2}{5}$ is less than $\frac{2}{4}$. Since $\frac{2}{4} = \frac{1}{2}$, it follows that $\frac{2}{5}$ is less than $\frac{1}{2}$.

3. Lee Yah is wrong.

4. Answers will vary; for example: If one cake is cut into 6 pieces, each piece is bigger than if the cake is cut into 8 pieces. When numerators are the same and denominators are different, the larger denominator makes a smaller fraction.

Fact Families for × and ÷

Complete the number sentences for the related facts.

A. 3 × 10 = ___

___ ÷ 3 = ___

___ ÷ 10 = ___

___ × 3 = ___

B. 3 × 7 = ___

___ ÷ 7 = ___

___ ÷ 3 = ___

7 × ___ = ___

C. 2 × 2 = ___

___ ÷ 2 = ___

D. 12 ÷ 6 = ___

___ × 6 = ___

12 ÷ ___ = ___

___ × 2 = ___

E. 3 × ___ = 9

9 ÷ ___ = ___

TIMS Bit

A. 30; 30 ÷ 3 = 10;
   30 ÷ 10 = 3;
   10 × 3 = 30

B. 21; 21 ÷ 7 = 3;
   21 ÷ 3 = 7;
   7 × 3 = 21

C. 4; 4 ÷ 2 = 2

D. 2; 2 × 6 = 12;
   12 ÷ 2 = 6;
   6 × 2 = 12

E. 3 × 3 = 9;
   9 ÷ 3 = 3

Trading Times

Use the following information to answer the questions below. Check to see if your answers are reasonable.

60 seconds = 1 minute   24 hours = 1 day
60 minutes = 1 hour   7 days = 1 week

1. 10 days = ? hours

2. 5 weeks = ? days

3. 20 hours = ? minutes

4. 30 minutes = ? seconds

5. $3\frac{1}{2}$ hours = ? minutes

6. 56 days = ? weeks

TIMS Task

1. 240 hours

2. 35 days

3. 1200 minutes

4. 1800 seconds

5. 210 minutes

6. 8 weeks

 Comparing Fractions

Which fractions below are:

$\frac{3}{5}$ $\frac{1}{10}$ $\frac{2}{4}$ $\frac{9}{8}$ $\frac{1}{3}$ $\frac{4}{5}$ $\frac{3}{6}$ $\frac{8}{12}$ $\frac{2}{6}$

1. Equal to $\frac{1}{2}$?

2. Less than $\frac{1}{2}$?

3. Greater than $\frac{1}{2}$?

TIMS Bit

Students can refer to the Number Lines for Fractohoppers chart in the *Student Guide* for Lesson 4.

1. $\frac{2}{4}$ and $\frac{3}{6}$

2. $\frac{1}{10}$, $\frac{1}{3}$, and $\frac{2}{6}$

3. $\frac{3}{5}$, $\frac{9}{8}$, $\frac{4}{5}$, and $\frac{8}{12}$

What's My Length?

TIMS Task

1. A. How many inches are in one foot?

   B. How many inches are in 5 feet?

   C. Name something that is about 1 inch long.

   D. Name something that is about 1 foot long.

2. A. How many feet are in one yard?

   B. How many yards is 24 feet?

   C. How many feet are in 6 yards?

   D. Name something that is about 1 yard long.

3. Which is longer, a yardstick or a meterstick? How much longer?

In Lesson 6 *Distance vs. Time*, students measure in yards. Students complete this task to explore other units of measurement for length. Encourage students to use tools in the classroom to help them answer the questions. Make sure yardsticks and metersticks are available.

1. A. 12 inches

   B. 60 inches

   C. Answers will vary: a small paper clip, the distance from your knuckle to the end of your thumb

   D. Answers will vary: a book, a computer screen

2. A. 3 feet

   B. 8 yards

   C. 18 feet

   D. Answers will vary: the height of the teacher's desk, a younger brother or sister

3. meterstick; about 3 inches longer

Choosing Units of Measure

The following are some units of measure for length: meters, centimeters, feet, inches, yards, kilometers, and miles.

Which unit of measure does it make sense to use when you measure:

1. the length of a book?

2. the distance from your classroom door to your teacher's desk?

3. the distance from your home to school?

4. a person's height?

TIMS Bit

Answers will vary.

1. centimeters, inches

2. feet, meters, centimeters, inches, yards

3. For some students who live across the street or around the corner, they might say feet or yards. Others who take the bus to school might say miles or kilometers.

4. feet and inches, centimeters

Subtracting Time

Jerome is traveling on a train. He is going to visit his aunt. The train ride is 4 hours and 30 minutes long. So far he has traveled for 2 hours and 45 minutes. Jerome wants to know how much longer the train ride is. He writes the following:

4 hours 30 minutes
−2 hours 45 minutes
‾‾‾‾‾‾‾‾‾‾‾‾‾‾‾‾‾‾‾

3 hours 90 minutes
−2 hours 45 minutes
‾‾‾‾‾‾‾‾‾‾‾‾‾‾‾‾‾‾‾
1 hour   45 minutes

Jerome still has 1 hour and 45 minutes left on his train ride.

1. Explain how Jerome changed 4 hours 30 minutes to 3 hours and 90 minutes. Why did he rewrite the problem?

2. Solve these problems.

   A. 7 hours 18 minutes – 4 hours 16 minutes

   B. 5 hours 26 minutes – 2 hours 36 minutes

   C. 12 hours 28 minutes – 6 hours 54 minutes

   D. 17 hours 47 minutes – 6 hours 50 minutes

TIMS Task

1. Jerome took 1 hour from the 4 hours and changed it to 60 minutes. Then, he added 60 minutes and 30 minutes to get 90 minutes. Now he can subtract 90 minutes – 45 minutes = 45 minutes.

2. A. 3 hours 2 minutes

   B. 2 hours and 50 minutes

   C. 5 hours and 34 minutes

   D. 10 hours and 57 minutes

Quiz: 2s and 3s

A. $3 \times 5 =$

B. $14 \div 2 =$

C. $18 \div 3 =$

D. $3 \times 10 =$

E. $2 \times 2 =$

F. $7 \times 3 =$

G. $12 \div 6 =$

H. $8 \div 4 =$

I. $12 \div 4 =$

J. $24 \div 3 =$

K. $9 \div 3 =$

L. $2 \times 9 =$

M. $9 \times 3 =$

N. $5 \times 2 =$

O. $16 \div 8 =$

P. $3 \times 2 =$

Q. $20 \div 2 =$

TIMS Bit

We recommend 5 minutes for this quiz. Allow students to change pens after the time is up and complete the remaining problems in a different color. After students take the test, have them update their *Multiplication Facts I Know* and *Division Facts I Know* charts.

Goldfish on Sale

1. Complete the table for the cost of fancy goldfish.

N Number of Goldfish	C Cost
2	$3.00
4	
	$7.50

2. Using fractions, write three other ratios that are equal to $\frac{\$3.00}{2 \text{ fish}}$.

3. How much will 3 dozen fancy goldfish cost?

TIMS Task

1.
N Number of Goldfish	C Cost
1	$1.50
2	$3.00
3	$4.50
4	$6.00
5	$7.50
6	$9.00

2. Answers will vary. One possible response is:
$$\frac{\$1.50}{1 \text{ fish}} = \frac{\$4.50}{3 \text{ fish}} = \frac{\$6.00}{4 \text{ fish}}$$

3. $54—Discuss students' strategies.

Lesson ① Wholes and Parts

Lesson Overview

Estimated Class Sessions 1-2

Students model fractions using pattern blocks. They use the blocks to define a whole unit and represent fractions of the whole. An activity from fourth grade is included for students who have not had previous experience using pattern blocks to model fractions.

Key Content

- Representing fractions using manipulatives and symbols.
- Finding a fraction for a given quantity when a unit whole is given.

Key Vocabulary

- denominator
- numerator

Math Facts

Review the multiplication and division facts for the 2s and 3s. Complete DPP item B.

Homework

1. Assign the *Homework: Wholes and Parts* Activity Pages found in the *Discovery Assignment Book*.
2. Assign Parts 1 and 2 of the Home Practice.

Assessment

Use the homework pages in the *Discovery Assignment Book* to assess students' abilities to represent a fraction given a whole.

Curriculum Sequence

Before This Unit

Fractions

Students explored fraction concepts in Grades 1–4. In third and fourth grade, students used paper folding and pattern blocks to model fractions. They studied the concept of a whole, comparing fractions, equivalent fractions, and modeling addition and subtraction of fractions with manipulatives. See Grade 4 Unit 12 *Exploring Fractions* for specific activities.

Decimals

Students explored decimals in Unit 10 of fourth grade. They will use decimals to solve a problem in this lesson.

After This Unit

Fractions

Students will continue to study fractions extensively in fifth grade. They will model fractions using pattern blocks, number lines, and rectangles on dot paper. Fraction concepts and computation will be connected to work with decimals, ratios, and proportions. Students review topics from fourth grade and learn paper-and-pencil procedures for adding, subtracting, and multiplying fractions. Units 5, 9, 11, and 12 deal specifically with fractions.

Decimals

Students will study decimals in Unit 7.

Materials List

Supplies and Copies

Student	Teacher
Supplies for Each Student Pair • 1 set of pattern blocks (2–3 yellow hexagons, 6 red trapezoids, 10 blue rhombuses, 10 green triangles, 6 brown trapezoids, 12 purple triangles)	**Supplies** • overhead pattern blocks, optional
Copies • 1 copy of *Introducing Pattern Block Fractions* per student, optional (*Unit Resource Guide* Pages 40–42)	**Copies/Transparencies** • 1 transparency of *Pattern Block Record Sheet* (*Discovery Assignment Book* Page 35)

All blackline masters including assessment, transparency, and DPP masters are also on the Teacher Resource CD.

Student Books
Wholes and Parts (*Student Guide* Pages 68–72)
Triangle Flash Cards: 2s (*Discovery Assignment Book* Page 31)
Triangle Flash Cards: 3s (*Discovery Assignment Book* Page 33)
Pattern Block Record Sheet (*Discovery Assignment Book* Page 35)
Homework: Wholes and Parts (*Discovery Assignment Book* Pages 37–38)

Daily Practice and Problems and Home Practice
DPP items A–B (*Unit Resource Guide* Pages 15–16)
Home Practice Parts 1–2 (*Discovery Assignment Book* Page 27)

Note: Classrooms whose pacing differs significantly from the suggested pacing of the units should use the Math Facts Calendar in Section 4 of the *Facts Resource Guide* to ensure students receive the complete math facts program.

Daily Practice and Problems

Suggestions for using the DPPs are on pages 37–38.

A. Bit: Number Changes (URG p. 15)

Always begin with the number: 5,987,654,321

Change it to:

A. 12 million more
B. 50 thousand less
C. 7 hundred more
D. 200 million more
E. 3 billion less

B. Task: Multiplication and Division Facts: 2s and 3s (URG p. 16)

With a partner, use your *Triangle Flash Cards* to quiz each other on the multiplication and division facts for the 2s and 3s. Follow the directions in the *Student Guide* for Unit 2 Lesson 2 *Facts I Know.*

As your partner quizzes you on the multiplication facts, separate the facts into three piles: those facts you know and can answer quickly, those you can figure out with a strategy, and those you need to learn. Practice any facts for the 2s and 3s that are in the last two piles. List these facts so you can practice them at home. Repeat the process for the division facts.

Circle all the facts you know and can answer quickly on your *Multiplication* and *Division Facts I Know* charts.

In this unit and in Unit 5 and Unit 12, students use the following pattern blocks: yellow hexagons, red trapezoids, blue rhombuses, green triangles, brown trapezoids, and purple triangles as shown in Figure 1. If the yellow hexagon is one whole, the red trapezoid is one-half, the blue rhombus is one-third, the green triangle is one-sixth, the brown trapezoid is one-fourth, and the purple triangle is one-twelfth.

The yellow hexagon, red trapezoid, blue rhombus, and green triangle are traditional pattern blocks. In third grade, students used these four blocks in their study of fractions. The brown trapezoid and purple triangle are sold separately as fraction pattern blocks. In fourth grade, students included the brown trapezoids in their study. In fifth grade, they use the purple triangles for the first time. During the fraction units, put together sets of pattern blocks for each pair of students as described in the materials section. Then store the sets in resealable plastic bags or plastic containers with lids. (Note that students will also use the orange square and tan rhombus pattern blocks during Unit 6 in their study of geometry.)

The *Introducing Pattern Block Fractions* Activity Pages in the *Unit Resource Guide* are taken from Grade 4 Unit 12 *Exploring Fractions.* Students who did not use pattern blocks in previous grades to model fractions can use these pages as an introduction. *Questions 1–12* acquaint students with the pattern blocks used in fourth grade and their relationships to one another. In *Questions 13–19* students name fractions when given the block (or blocks) that represents one whole. They also name the whole when given a fraction. Note that *Question 15C* asks students to show a fraction greater than one ($\frac{5}{4}$) and *Questions 17E–17F* ask students to name fractions greater than one. In this activity, students can either write fractions greater than one as mixed numbers or improper fractions. For example, the answer to *Question 17E* can either be written as $\frac{3}{2}$ or $1\frac{1}{2}$. In *Questions 20–26* students model easy addition problems using pattern blocks. Although they do not learn pencil-and-paper procedures for adding unlike fractions until a later unit, using manipulatives provides students with a strategy for adding unlike fractions without finding common denominators. For example, *Question 22* asks them to show one whole (the yellow hexagon) using two or more colors and then write a fraction sentence. Figure 2 shows possible solutions.

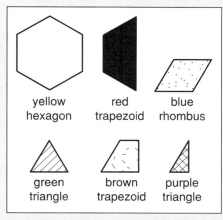

Figure 1: *Pattern blocks used in fifth grade to model fractions*

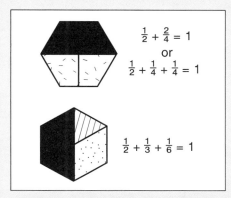

$$\frac{1}{2} + \frac{2}{4} = 1$$
or
$$\frac{1}{2} + \frac{1}{4} + \frac{1}{4} = 1$$

$$\frac{1}{2} + \frac{1}{3} + \frac{1}{6} = 1$$

Figure 2: *Number sentences for one whole*

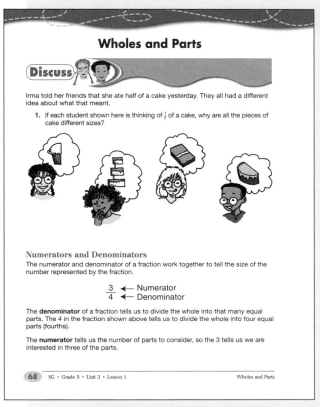

Wholes and Parts

Discuss

Irma told her friends that she ate half of a cake yesterday. They all had a different idea about what that meant.

1. If each student shown here is thinking of $\frac{1}{2}$ of a cake, why are all the pieces of cake different sizes?

Numerators and Denominators

The numerator and denominator of a fraction work together to tell the size of the number represented by the fraction.

$$\frac{3}{4}$$ ← Numerator
← Denominator

The **denominator** of a fraction tells us to divide the whole into that many equal parts. The 4 in the fraction shown above tells us to divide the whole into four equal parts (fourths).

The **numerator** tells us the number of parts to consider, so the 3 tells us we are interested in three of the parts.

68   SG • Grade 5 • Unit 3 • Lesson 1   Wholes and Parts

Student Guide - page 68 *(Answers on p. 43)*

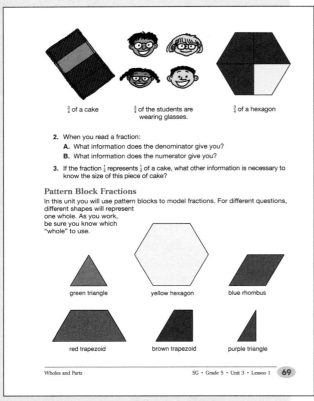

³⁄₄ of a cake   ³⁄₄ of the students are   ³⁄₄ of a hexagon
wearing glasses.

2. When you read a fraction:
   A. What information does the denominator give you?
   B. What information does the numerator give you?

3. If the fraction ¼ represents ¼ of a cake, what other information is necessary to know the size of this piece of cake?

Pattern Block Fractions
In this unit you will use pattern blocks to model fractions. For different questions, different shapes will represent one whole. As you work, be sure you know which "whole" to use.

green triangle   yellow hexagon   blue rhombus

red trapezoid   brown trapezoid   purple triangle

Wholes and Parts   SG • Grade 5 • Unit 3 • Lesson 1   **69**

Student Guide - page 69 *(Answers on p. 43)*

---

4. A. Cover a green triangle with purple triangles. How many purple triangles do you need?
   B. How many green triangles cover one yellow hexagon?

5. A. Cover a yellow hexagon with purple triangles. How many purple triangles do you need?
   B. Cover a brown trapezoid with purple triangles. How many purple triangles make the same shape as a brown trapezoid?

6. A. How many brown trapezoids cover a red trapezoid?

1 whole

   B. If the red trapezoid is one whole, which block models ½?
   C. If the red trapezoid is one whole, which block models ⅙?
   D. If the red trapezoid is one whole, which block models ⅓?
   E. If the red trapezoid is one whole, which block models 2?

70   SG • Grade 5 • Unit 3 • Lesson 1   Wholes and Parts

Student Guide - page 70 *(Answers on p. 44)*

Teaching the Activity

Use the illustration and questions on the *Wholes and Parts* Activity Pages in the *Student Guide* to begin the lesson. *Questions 1–2* review fraction concepts. In *Question 1* students discuss the concept of a whole. When using fractions to represent parts of a whole, it is necessary to know the size of the whole unit. The picture on the *Student Guide* page illustrates this point. All the students imagine cakes of different sizes, so each half of a cake is also a different size. *Question 2* reviews the terms numerator and denominator.

Students work in pairs to answer *Questions 3–13.* These questions introduce the purple pattern block while reviewing the rest of the blocks and their relationships to one another. Note that the purple and brown pattern blocks are harder to use than the other blocks. Students may need to flip or rotate some of them in order to cover another block. If students have trouble manipulating these blocks, they can use the *Pattern Block Record Sheet* from the *Discovery Assignment Book* to help them orient the blocks. Figure 3 shows a hexagon as shown on the *Pattern Block Record Sheet.* Dotted lines outline the placement of the purple pattern blocks.

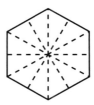

Figure 3: *Hexagon from the* Pattern Block Record Sheet

Questions 7–13 ask students to model various fractions when given a whole, and give the whole when given a fraction. Note that *Question 12* reviews the use of decimals to write tenths. Students will need their *Pattern Block Record Sheet* to complete *Question 13.* Students shade fractions on the printed hexagons. This prepares them for the homework pages in the *Discovery Assignment Book.*

Content Note

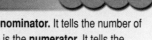

In the fraction ⅝, the 8 is the **denominator.** It tells the number of equal parts in the whole. The 5 is the **numerator.** It tells the number of parts being considered.

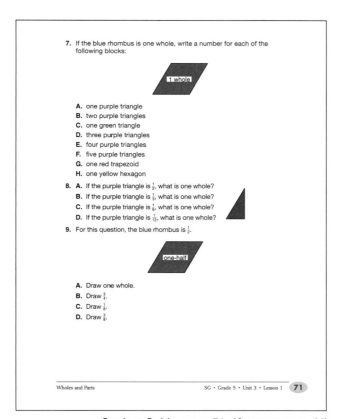

Student Guide - page 71 *(Answers on p. 44)*

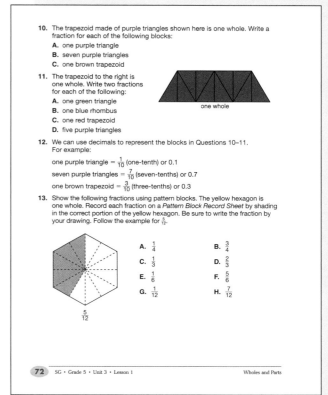

Student Guide - page 72 *(Answers on p. 45)*

Journal Prompt

John said, "I ate $\frac{1}{4}$ of a pizza with my family last night." Michael said, "I ate $\frac{1}{4}$ of a pizza at a party last night." Did they eat the same amount of pizza? Explain.

Math Facts

Use DPP item B to begin the review of the multiplication and division facts for the 2s and 3s.

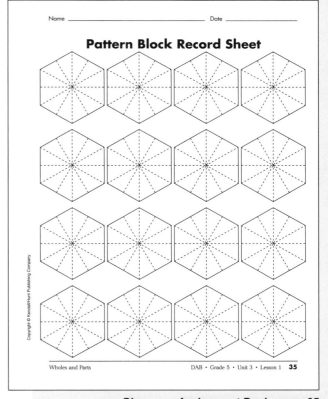

Discovery Assignment Book - page 35

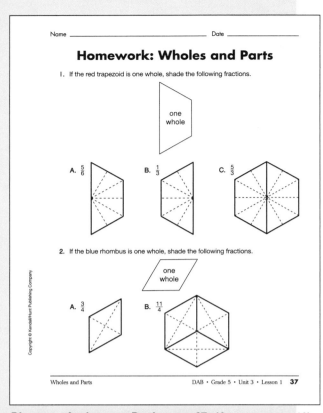

Discovery Assignment Book - page 37 *(Answers on p. 46)*

- The *Homework: Wholes and Parts* Activity Pages in the *Discovery Assignment Book* provide more practice representing fractions given the whole. Students shade in drawings of pattern blocks to show the fractions.
- Use DPP Bit A to practice number sense skills with big numbers.
- Assign Parts 1 and 2 in the Home Practice.

Answers for Parts 1 and 2 of the Home Practice are in the Answer Key at the end of this lesson and at the end of this unit.

Assessment

Use the *Homework: Wholes and Parts* Activity Pages in the *Discovery Assignment Book* to assess students' abilities to represent a fraction when given a whole.

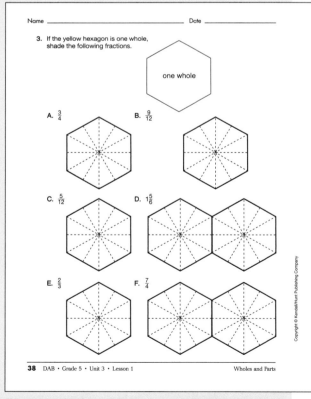

Discovery Assignment Book - page 38 *(Answers on p. 47)*

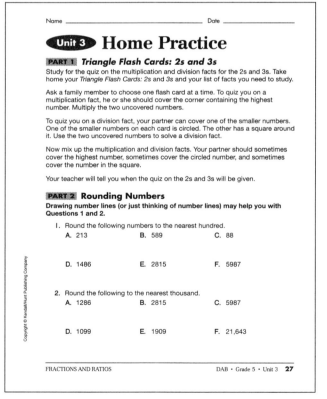

Discovery Assignment Book - page 27 *(Answers on p. 46)*

At a Glance

Math Facts and Daily Practice and Problems

1. Review the multiplication and division facts for the 2s and 3s. Complete DPP item B.
2. Use Bit A to improve students' number sense.

Before the Activity

1. Organize the pattern blocks into sets for each pair of students as described in the materials section of the Lesson Guide.
2. If students have no previous experience using pattern blocks to model fractions, they can complete the *Introducing Pattern Block Fractions* Activity Pages in the *Unit Resource Guide.* These pages are taken from a fourth grade lesson.

Teaching the Activity

1. Using *Questions 1–2* on the *Wholes and Parts* Activity Pages in the *Student Guide,* students review the terms numerator and denominator along with the concept that it is necessary to define the whole unit before the size of a fraction can be determined.
2. Working in pairs, students review the use of pattern blocks to model fractions as they are introduced to the purple triangle *(Questions 3–5).*
3. Students answer *Questions 3–12* using pattern blocks.
4. Students use a *Pattern Block Record Sheet* from the *Discovery Assignment Book* to answer *Question 13.*

Homework

1. Assign the *Homework: Wholes and Parts* Activity Pages found in the *Discovery Assignment Book.*
2. Assign Parts 1 and 2 of the Home Practice.

Assessment

Use the homework pages in the *Discovery Assignment Book* to assess students' abilities to represent a fraction given a whole.

Answer Key is on pages 43–50.

Notes:

Introducing
Pattern Block Fractions

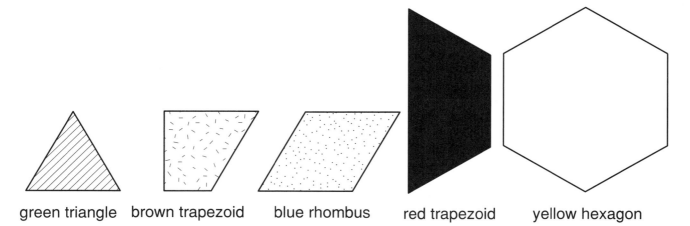

green triangle   brown trapezoid   blue rhombus   red trapezoid   yellow hexagon

**Cover each pattern block shape shown here with the correct pattern block.
Use your set of pattern blocks to help you answer the following questions:**

1. How many blue rhombuses cover one yellow hexagon?

2. How many brown trapezoids cover one yellow hexagon?

3. How many brown trapezoids cover one red trapezoid?

4. How many red trapezoids cover one yellow hexagon?

5. The area of one brown trapezoid is (less than, greater than, or equal to) the area of one red trapezoid?

6. How many brown trapezoids cover three red trapezoids?

7. The area of one brown trapezoid is (less than, greater than, or equal to) the area of one green triangle?

8. How many green triangles cover one yellow hexagon?

9. Two brown trapezoids plus how many green triangles cover one yellow hexagon? Show your solution in a picture.

10. How many green triangles cover two brown trapezoids?

11. How many green triangles cover two blue rhombuses?

12. The area of two blue rhombuses is (less than, greater than, or equal to) the area of one brown trapezoid?

Exploring Fractions

13. Each of these figures shows thirds ($\frac{1}{3}$s) using pattern blocks. This means a shape is divided into three equal parts. Build these figures with pattern blocks. Place three blue rhombuses on a yellow hexagon. Place three green triangles on a red trapezoid.

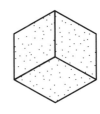 

  A. If the red trapezoid is one whole, which block shows $\frac{1}{3}$?

  B. If the blue rhombus is $\frac{1}{3}$, which block shows one whole?

  C. If the red trapezoid is one whole, show $\frac{2}{3}$.

14. A. If the yellow hexagon is one whole, which block shows $\frac{1}{2}$?

  B. If the red trapezoid is one whole, which block shows $\frac{1}{2}$?

  C. If the green triangle is $\frac{1}{2}$, which block is one whole?

15. A. If the yellow hexagon is one whole, which block shows $\frac{1}{4}$?

  B. If the yellow hexagon is one whole, show $\frac{3}{4}$.

  C. If the yellow hexagon is one whole, show $\frac{5}{4}$.

16. A. If the green triangle is $\frac{1}{6}$, which block is one whole?

  B. If the yellow hexagon is one whole, show $\frac{3}{6}$.

  C. If the yellow hexagon is one whole, show $\frac{5}{6}$.

17. If the red trapezoid is one whole, name each of the following fractions:

  A. one green triangle

  B. two green triangles

  C. one blue rhombus

  D. one brown trapezoid

  E. three brown trapezoids

  F. five green triangles

18. The large hexagon shown to the right is one whole.

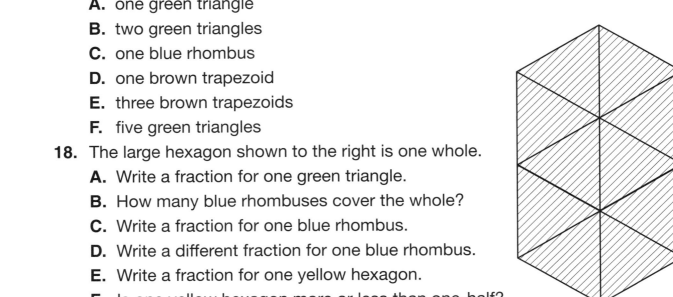

  A. Write a fraction for one green triangle.

  B. How many blue rhombuses cover the whole?

  C. Write a fraction for one blue rhombus.

  D. Write a different fraction for one blue rhombus.

  E. Write a fraction for one yellow hexagon.

  F. Is one yellow hexagon more or less than one-half?

19. If the yellow hexagon is one whole, name each of the following fractions:

A. one red trapezoid

B. one brown trapezoid

C. two brown trapezoids

D. one blue rhombus

E. two green triangles

F. two blue rhombuses

G. three red trapezoids

one whole

Fraction Sentences

For Questions 20–26, the yellow hexagon is one whole. The red trapezoid is $\frac{1}{2}$. We can show $\frac{1}{2}$ using brown blocks. Since 1 red trapezoid equals 2 brown trapezoids, then $\frac{1}{2} = \frac{2}{4}$ or $\frac{1}{2} = \frac{1}{4} + \frac{1}{4}$.

20. Show $\frac{1}{2}$ using green blocks. (Cover a red trapezoid with green blocks.) Write a number sentence to represent this figure.

21. The blue rhombus is $\frac{1}{3}$. Show $\frac{1}{3}$ using green blocks and write a number sentence to represent this figure.

We can show 1 whole with two or more colors and write a number sentence to represent the figure.

$$1 = \frac{1}{3} + \frac{1}{3} + \frac{1}{6} + \frac{1}{6}$$

or

$$1 = \frac{2}{3} + \frac{2}{6}$$

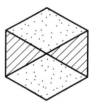

22. Show 1 whole another way using two or more colors. Write a number sentence for your figure.

For Questions 23–26, show each fraction using two or more colors. The yellow hexagon is one whole. Write a number sentence for each figure.

23. Show $\frac{1}{2}$.

24. Show $\frac{3}{4}$.

25. Show $\frac{2}{3}$.

26. Show $\frac{3}{2}$.

Student Guide (p. 68)

Wholes and Parts

1. Answers will vary. Each whole cake is a different size.*

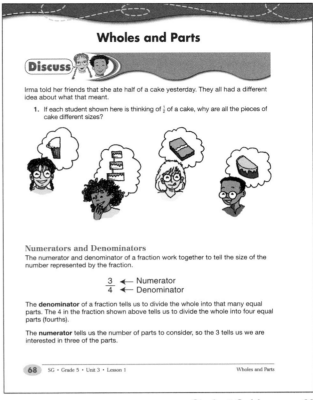

Student Guide - page 68

Student Guide (p. 69)

2. **A.** The denominator tells you how many pieces the whole is divided into.

   B. The numerator tells you how many pieces of the whole you are interested in.

   C. You need to know the size of the whole.

3. **A.** 2 purple triangles

   B. 6 green triangles

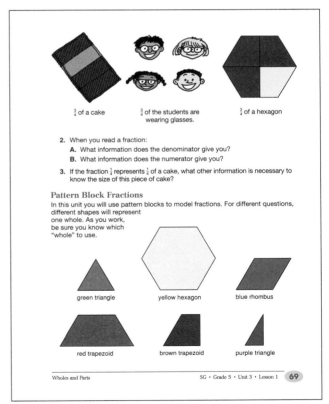

Student Guide - page 69

*Answers and/or discussion are included in the Lesson Guide.

4. A. Cover a green triangle with purple triangles. How many purple triangles do you need?

B. How many green triangles cover one yellow hexagon?

5. A. Cover a yellow hexagon with purple triangles. How many purple triangles do you need?

B. Cover a brown trapezoid with purple triangles. How many purple triangles make the same shape as a brown trapezoid?

6. A. How many brown trapezoids cover a red trapezoid?

1 whole

B. If the red trapezoid is one whole, which block models $\frac{1}{2}$?
C. If the red trapezoid is one whole, which block models $\frac{1}{6}$?
D. If the red trapezoid is one whole, which block models $\frac{1}{3}$?
E. If the red trapezoid is one whole, which block models 2?

Student Guide - page 70

Student Guide (p. 70)

4. 12 purple triangles

5. 3 purple triangles

6. A. 2 brown trapezoids

    B. brown trapezoid

    C. purple triangle

    D. green triangle

    E. yellow hexagon

---

7. If the blue rhombus is one whole, write a number for each of the following blocks:

1 whole

A. one purple triangle
B. two purple triangles
C. one green triangle
D. three purple triangles
E. four purple triangles
F. five purple triangles
G. one red trapezoid
H. one yellow hexagon

8. A. If the purple triangle is $\frac{1}{2}$, what is one whole?
B. If the purple triangle is $\frac{1}{3}$, what is one whole?
C. If the purple triangle is $\frac{1}{6}$, what is one whole?
D. If the purple triangle is $\frac{1}{12}$, what is one whole?

9. For this question, the blue rhombus is $\frac{1}{2}$.

one-half

A. Draw one whole.
B. Draw $\frac{3}{4}$.
C. Draw $\frac{1}{8}$.
D. Draw $\frac{3}{8}$.

Student Guide - page 71

Student Guide (p. 71)

7. A. $\frac{1}{4}$ **B.** $\frac{2}{4}$ or $\frac{1}{2}$

    C. $\frac{1}{2}$ **D.** $\frac{3}{4}$

    E. 1 or $\frac{4}{4}$ **F.** $1\frac{1}{4}$ or $\frac{5}{4}$

    G. $1\frac{1}{2}$ or $\frac{3}{2}$ **H.** 3

8. A. green triangle

    B. brown trapezoid

    C. red trapezoid

    D. yellow hexagon

9. A.   **B.**

    C.   **D.**

Student Guide (p. 72)

10. **A.** $\frac{1}{10}$

 B. $\frac{7}{10}$

 C. $\frac{3}{10}$

11. **A.** $\frac{1}{5}$ and $\frac{2}{10}$

 B. $\frac{2}{5}$ and $\frac{4}{10}$

 C. $\frac{3}{5}$ and $\frac{6}{10}$

 D. $\frac{1}{2}$ and $\frac{5}{10}$

12. **A.** One green triangle is 0.2. **B.** One blue rhombus is 0.4. **C.** One red trapezoid is 0.6. **D.** five purple triangles is 0.5.

13. **A.** $\frac{1}{4}$

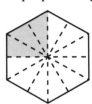

 B. $\frac{3}{4}$

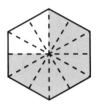

 C. $\frac{1}{3}$

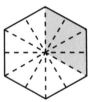

 D. $\frac{2}{3}$

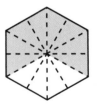

 E. $\frac{1}{6}$

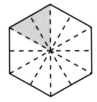

 F. $\frac{5}{6}$

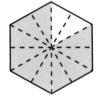

 G. $\frac{1}{12}$

 H. $\frac{7}{12}$

---

10. The trapezoid made of purple triangles shown here is one whole. Write a fraction for each of the following blocks:
 A. one purple triangle
 B. seven purple triangles
 C. one brown trapezoid

11. The trapezoid to the right is one whole. Write two fractions for each of the following:
 A. one green triangle
 B. one blue rhombus
 C. one red trapezoid
 D. five purple triangles

one whole

12. We can use decimals to represent the blocks in Questions 10–11. For example:
 one purple triangle = $\frac{1}{10}$ (one-tenth) or 0.1
 seven purple triangles = $\frac{7}{10}$ (seven-tenths) or 0.7
 one brown trapezoid = $\frac{3}{10}$ (three-tenths) or 0.3

13. Show the following fractions using pattern blocks. The yellow hexagon is one whole. Record each fraction on a *Pattern Block Record Sheet* by shading in the correct portion of the yellow hexagon. Be sure to write the fraction by your drawing. Follow the example for $\frac{5}{12}$.

A. $\frac{1}{4}$	**B.** $\frac{3}{4}$
C. $\frac{1}{3}$	**D.** $\frac{2}{3}$
E. $\frac{1}{6}$	**F.** $\frac{5}{6}$
G. $\frac{1}{12}$	**H.** $\frac{7}{12}$

$\frac{5}{12}$

Student Guide - page 72

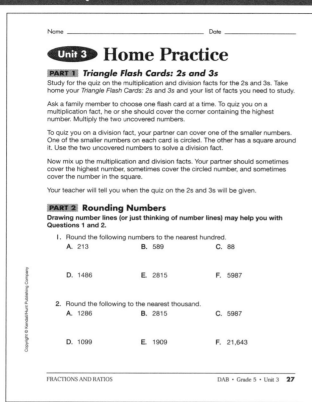

Discovery Assignment Book - page 27

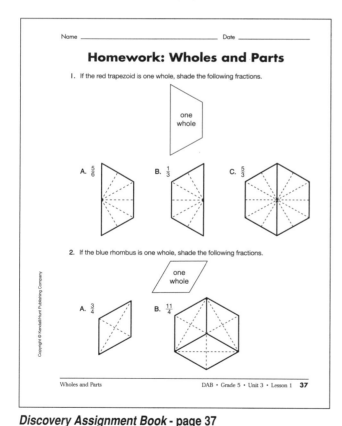

Discovery Assignment Book - page 37

Discovery Assignment Book (p. 27)

Home Practice*

Part 2. Rounding Numbers

1. A. 200
    B. 600
    C. 100
    D. 1500
    E. 2800
    F. 6000

2. A. 1000
    B. 3000
    C. 6000
    D. 1000
    E. 2000
    F. 22,000

Discovery Assignment Book (p. 37)

Homework: Wholes and Parts

1. A.
    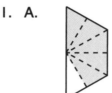

    B.
    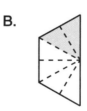

    C.
    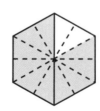

2. A.
    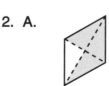

    B.
    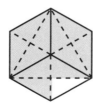

*Answers for all the Home Practice in the *Discovery Assignment Book* are at the end of the unit.

Discovery Assignment Book (p. 38)

3. A.

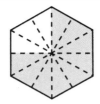

B.

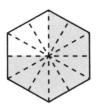

C.

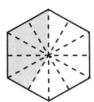

D.

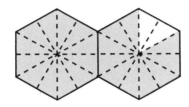

E.

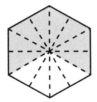

F.

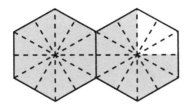

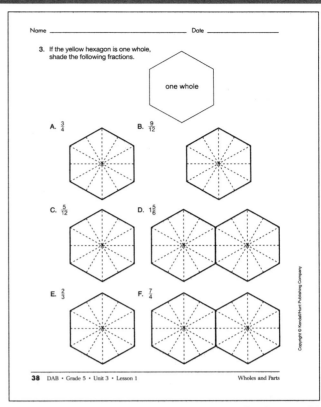

Name _____   Date _____

3. If the yellow hexagon is one whole, shade the following fractions.

one whole

A. $\frac{3}{4}$ B. $\frac{9}{12}$

C. $\frac{5}{12}$ D. $1\frac{5}{6}$

E. $\frac{2}{3}$ F. $\frac{7}{4}$

Copyright © Kendall/Hunt Publishing Company

Discovery Assignment Book - page 38

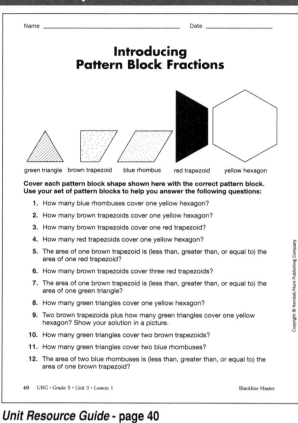

Unit Resource Guide - page 40

Unit Resource Guide (p. 40)

Introducing Pattern Block Fractions

1. 3 blue rhombuses
2. 4 brown trapezoids
3. 2 brown trapezoids
4. 2 red trapezoids
5. less than
6. 6 brown trapezoids
7. greater than
8. 6 green triangles
9. 3 green triangles
10. 3 green triangles
11. 4 green triangles
12. greater than

Unit Resource Guide (p. 41)

13. **A.** green triangle
    B. yellow hexagon
    C.

14. **A.** red trapezoid
    B. brown trapezoid
    C. blue rhombus

15. **A.** brown trapezoid
    B.
    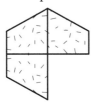

    C.
    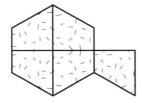

16. **A.** yellow hexagon
    B.

    C.

17. **A.** $\frac{1}{3}$
    B. $\frac{2}{3}$
    C. $\frac{2}{3}$
    D. $\frac{1}{2}$
    E. $1\frac{1}{2}$ or $\frac{3}{2}$
    F. $1\frac{2}{3}$ or $\frac{5}{3}$

18. **A.** $\frac{1}{10}$
    B. 5
    C. $\frac{1}{5}$ or $\frac{2}{10}$
    D. $\frac{2}{10}$ or $\frac{1}{5}$
    E. $\frac{3}{5}$ or $\frac{6}{10}$
    F. more

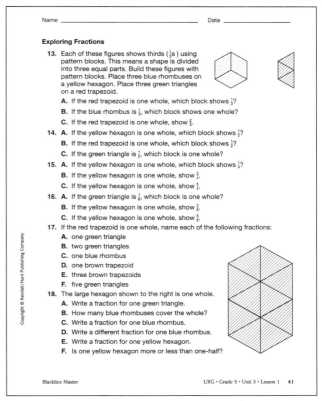

Exploring Fractions

13. Each of these figures shows thirds ($\frac{1}{3}$s) using pattern blocks. This means a shape is divided into three equal parts. Build these figures with pattern blocks. Place three blue rhombuses on a yellow hexagon. Place three green triangles on a red trapezoid.
    A. If the red trapezoid is one whole, which block shows $\frac{1}{3}$?
    B. If the blue rhombus is $\frac{1}{3}$, which block shows one whole?
    C. If the red trapezoid is one whole, show $\frac{2}{3}$.
14. **A.** If the yellow hexagon is one whole, which block shows $\frac{1}{2}$?
    B. If the red trapezoid is one whole, which block shows $\frac{1}{2}$?
    C. If the green triangle is $\frac{1}{2}$, which block is one whole?
15. **A.** If the yellow hexagon is one whole, which block shows $\frac{1}{4}$?
    B. If the yellow hexagon is one whole, show $\frac{3}{4}$.
    C. If the yellow hexagon is one whole, show $\frac{5}{4}$.
16. **A.** If the green triangle is $\frac{1}{6}$, which block is one whole?
    B. If the yellow hexagon is one whole, show $\frac{2}{3}$.
    C. If the yellow hexagon is one whole, show $\frac{5}{6}$.
17. If the red trapezoid is one whole, name each of the following fractions:
    A. one green triangle
    B. two green triangles
    C. one blue rhombus
    D. one brown trapezoid
    E. three brown trapezoids
    F. five green triangles
18. The large hexagon shown to the right is one whole.
    A. Write a fraction for one green triangle.
    B. How many blue rhombuses cover the whole?
    C. Write a fraction for one blue rhombus.
    D. Write a different fraction for one blue rhombus.
    E. Write a fraction for one yellow hexagon.
    F. Is one yellow hexagon more or less than one-half?

Blackline Master   URG • Grade 5 • Unit 3 • Lesson 1   41

Unit Resource Guide - page 41

Name _____ Date _____

19. If the yellow hexagon is one whole, name each of the following fractions:
    A. one red trapezoid
    B. one brown trapezoid
    C. two brown trapezoids
    D. one blue rhombus
    E. two green triangles
    F. two blue rhombuses
    G. three red trapezoids

one whole

Fraction Sentences
For Questions 20–26, the yellow hexagon is one whole. The red trapezoid is $\frac{1}{2}$.
We can show $\frac{1}{2}$ using brown blocks. Since 1 red trapezoid equals 2 brown
trapezoids, then $\frac{1}{2} = \frac{2}{4}$ or $\frac{1}{2} = \frac{1}{4} + \frac{1}{4}$.

20. Show $\frac{1}{2}$ using green blocks. (Cover a red trapezoid with green blocks.) Write a
    number sentence to represent this figure.

21. The blue rhombus is $\frac{1}{3}$. Show $\frac{1}{3}$ using green blocks and write a number
    sentence to represent this figure.

We can show 1 whole with two or more colors
and write a number sentence to represent
the figure.

$1 = \frac{1}{3} + \frac{1}{3} + \frac{1}{6} + \frac{1}{6}$
or
$1 = \frac{2}{3} + \frac{2}{6}$

22. Show 1 whole another way using two or
    more colors. Write a number sentence
    for your figure.

For Questions 23–26, show each fraction using two or more colors. The yellow
hexagon is one whole. Write a number sentence for each figure.

23. Show $\frac{1}{2}$.   24. Show $\frac{3}{4}$.
25. Show $\frac{2}{3}$.   26. Show $\frac{3}{2}$.

42   URG • Grade 5 • Unit 3 • Lesson 1   Blackline Master

Unit Resource Guide - page 42

Unit Resource Guide (p. 42)

19. A. $\frac{1}{2}$
    B. $\frac{1}{4}$
    C. $\frac{1}{2}$ or $\frac{2}{4}$
    D. $\frac{1}{3}$
    E. $\frac{1}{3}$ or $\frac{2}{6}$
    F. $\frac{2}{3}$
    G. $1\frac{1}{2}$ or $\frac{3}{2}$

20. $\frac{1}{6} + \frac{1}{6} + \frac{1}{6} = \frac{1}{2}$ or $\frac{3}{6} = \frac{1}{2}$

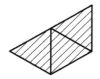

21. $\frac{1}{6} + \frac{1}{6} = \frac{1}{3}$ or $\frac{2}{6} = \frac{1}{3}$

22. Answers will vary. One possible solution is
    $\frac{1}{4} + \frac{1}{4} + \frac{1}{6} + \frac{1}{6} + \frac{1}{6} = 1$. See Figure 2 in Lesson
    Guide 1 for 2 additional answers.*

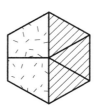

Answers will vary for *Questions 23–26.* One possible solution is shown for each.

23. $\frac{1}{3} + \frac{1}{6} = \frac{1}{2}$

24. $\frac{3}{6} + \frac{1}{4} = \frac{3}{4}$

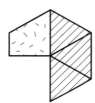

25. $\frac{1}{3} + \frac{1}{6} + \frac{1}{6} = \frac{2}{3}$

26. $\frac{1}{3} + \frac{1}{3} + \frac{1}{6} + \frac{1}{6} + \frac{1}{4} + \frac{1}{4} = \frac{3}{2}$

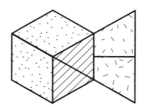

*Answers and/or discussion are included in the Lesson Guide.

Lesson 2

Fraction Sentences

Lesson Overview

Estimated Class Sessions 1-2

This lesson has two parts. In Part 1, students make figures using pattern blocks and represent their figures using number sentences. In Part 2, students explore fractions greater than one using pattern blocks and fraction sentences. They develop procedures for writing a mixed number as an improper fraction and an improper fraction as a mixed number.

Key Content

- Writing number sentences using fractions.
- Representing fractions greater than one with pattern blocks.
- Writing improper fractions as mixed numbers.
- Writing mixed numbers as improper fractions.

Key Vocabulary

- improper fraction
- mixed number
- proper fraction

Math Facts

Review the multiplication and division facts for the 2s and 3s. Complete DPP items C and D.

Homework

1. Assign the Homework section in the *Student Guide*.
2. Assign Part 4 of the Home Practice.

Curriculum Sequence

Before This Unit

In fourth grade students modeled easy addition and subtraction problems with fractions using pattern blocks and then wrote corresponding number sentences. See Lesson 6 *Pattern Block Fractions* and the open-ended assessment problem in Lesson 8 *Fraction Puzzles* in Grade 4 Unit 12 *Exploring Fractions.*

After This Unit

Students model addition and subtraction problems with fractions using rectangles on dot paper in Unit 5. They write appropriate number sentences. Using this new model, they explore using common denominators to add and subtract fractions. After work with common multiples in Unit 11, they formalize paper-and-pencil procedures for adding and subtracting fractions in Unit 12. Also in Unit 12, students model multiplication problems using paper folding and pattern blocks. Then they learn paper-and-pencil procedures for multiplying fractions.

Materials List

Supplies and Copies

Student	Teacher
Supplies for Each Student Pair • 1 set of pattern blocks (2–3 yellow hexagons, 6 red trapezoids, 10 blue rhombuses, 10 green triangles, 6 brown trapezoids, 12 purple triangles)	**Supplies** • overhead pattern blocks, optional
Copies • 1 copy of *Pattern Block Record Sheet* per student, optional (*Discovery Assignment Book* Page 35)	**Copies/Transparencies**

All blackline masters including assessment, transparency, and DPP masters are also on the Teacher Resource CD.

Student Books

Fraction Sentences (*Student Guide* Pages 73–76)
Pattern Block Record Sheet (*Discovery Assignment Book* Page 35), optional

Daily Practice and Problems and Home Practice

DPP items C–D (*Unit Resource Guide* Page 17)
Home Practice Part 4 (*Discovery Assignment Book* Page 28)

Note: Classrooms whose pacing differs significantly from the suggested pacing of the units should use the Math Facts Calendar in Section 4 of the *Facts Resource Guide* to ensure students receive the complete math facts program.

Daily Practice and Problems

Suggestions for using the DPPs are on page 57.

C. Bit: Multiplying by 10s
(URG p. 17)

A. 30 × 20 =   B. 80 × 30 =
C. 200 × 60 =   D. 50 × 300 =
E. 1000 × 30 =   F. 900 × 200 =
G. 6000 × 300 =   H. 20 × 200 =
I. 7000 × 3 =

D. Challenge: Bikes and Trikes
(URG p. 17)

There are some bicycles and some tricycles in the TIMS warehouse. The total number of wheels is 35.

1. How many bikes and how many trikes might be in the TIMS warehouse?
   (Give several answers to this problem.)
2. What is the fewest number of bikes that can be in the warehouse? Then how many trikes will there be?
3. What is the fewest number of trikes that can be in the warehouse? Then how many bikes will there be?
4. If the warehouse has a total of 15 bikes and trikes altogether, how many of each are in the warehouse?
5. If the number of bikes and trikes is the same, how many of each are in the warehouse?

Student Guide Page 73

Fraction Sentences

Mr. Moreno gave his class this challenge: Show one whole using three colors of blocks. Then write a number sentence for your figure. For this lesson, the yellow hexagon is one whole.

one whole

David and Brandon work together. Here is their figure.

Here is David's number sentence: $1 = \frac{3}{12} + \frac{1}{4} + \frac{1}{2}$

Here is Brandon's number sentence: $1 = \frac{1}{12} + \frac{1}{12} + \frac{1}{12} + \frac{1}{4} + \frac{1}{2}$

1. Show one whole a different way using three colors of blocks. Write a number sentence for your figure.

2. Lin shows $\frac{1}{2}$ using two colors. First, she shows $\frac{1}{2}$ with a red trapezoid. Then she trades blocks until she has the figure she wants.

   She represents her figure with this number sentence: $\frac{1}{2} = \frac{1}{6} + \frac{1}{6} + \frac{1}{12} + \frac{1}{12}$

   A. Write another number sentence for Lin's figure.
   B. Show $\frac{1}{2}$ a different way using two colors. Write a number sentence for your figure.

Fraction Sentences   SG • Grade 5 • Unit 3 • Lesson 2   **73**

Student Guide - page 73 *(Answers on p. 59)*

Student Guide Page 74

Explore

For Questions 3–8, show the fraction. Then write a number sentence for your figure. Remember, the yellow hexagon is one whole.

3. Show $\frac{1}{2}$ using brown and two other colors.

4. Show $\frac{3}{4}$ using brown and two other colors. (*Hint:* Show $\frac{3}{4}$ with three browns first. Then, either cover the brown pieces or trade pieces.)

5. Show $\frac{5}{6}$ using purple, green, and blue.

6. Show $\frac{2}{3}$ without using blue.

7. A. Show one whole using one color. (Use any color but yellow.)
   B. Show one whole using a different color.
   C. What can you say about the numerator and denominator of a fraction that is equal to 1?

8. Show $\frac{5}{6}$ using two colors.

Fractions Greater Than One

Ana shows $\frac{5}{3}$ using one color and writes these number sentences:

$\frac{5}{3} = \frac{1}{3} + \frac{1}{3} + \frac{1}{3} + \frac{1}{3} + \frac{1}{3}$

$5 \times \frac{1}{3} = \frac{5}{3}$

When the numerator is greater than or equal to the denominator, the fraction is called an **improper fraction**. Both $\frac{5}{3}$ and $\frac{3}{3}$ are improper fractions. When the numerator is less than the denominator, such as $\frac{2}{3}$, the fraction is called a **proper fraction**.

Manny shows $\frac{5}{3}$ using yellow and blue and writes these number sentences:

$\frac{5}{3} = 1 + \frac{2}{3}$

$\frac{5}{3} = 1\frac{2}{3}$

Numbers that are made up of a whole number and a fraction are called **mixed numbers**. $1\frac{2}{3}$ is a mixed number.

74   SG • Grade 5 • Unit 3 • Lesson 2   Fraction Sentences

Student Guide - page 74 *(Answers on p. 60)*

Teaching the Activity

Part 1 Fraction Sentences

The *Fraction Sentences* Activity Pages begin with examples of number sentences for one whole modeled with pattern blocks. ***Question 1*** asks students to show one whole another way using three colors and write number sentences for their figures. Figures 4 and 5 show two possible solutions and corresponding number sentences.

$$1 = \frac{1}{2} + \frac{1}{3} + \frac{2}{12}$$

Figure 4: *A number sentence for one whole*

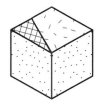

$$1 = \frac{1}{12} + \frac{1}{4} + \frac{1}{3} + \frac{1}{3}$$

Figure 5: *Another number sentence for one whole*

Students work in pairs to build figures and write number sentences. As students work, check their number sentences to see if they correspond to their figures. For example, be sure the sums really do equal one whole. Also, students should not use denominators that are not represented in their figures. For example, although $\frac{2}{12} = \frac{1}{6}$, the two purple triangles in Figure 4 should be represented in the number sentence by $\frac{2}{12}$ or $\frac{1}{12} + \frac{1}{12}$ and not by $\frac{1}{6}$.

In ***Questions 2–8,*** students build models of fractions according to specific criteria and write number sentences for their figures. Students' models for a given

---

TIMS Tip

If students have trouble making figures and orienting the blocks correctly, they can use the *Pattern Block Record Sheet* to help them. This may be easier than trying to lay the small pieces on top of the yellow hexagon pattern block.

---

fraction will differ from one another. When student pairs finish *Question 8,* ask them to join with another student pair to share their solutions and check number sentences.

Discuss *Question 7* with the class. Students represent one whole with one color, so they can show one whole as $\frac{2}{2}, \frac{3}{3}, \frac{4}{4}, \frac{6}{6}$, and $\frac{12}{12}$. Using these fractions as a guide, ask students to write one whole with various denominators such as 5, 50, and 500. They should recognize that fractions with the same numerator and denominator are equal to one whole.

Part 2 Fractions Greater Than One

Begin with the diagrams in the Fractions Greater Than One section in the *Student Guide.* Draw these two figures on the board or build them with overhead pattern blocks. Alternatively, you can show two other figures that model an improper fraction and the equivalent mixed number. Ask students to write number sentences for each of your figures. Since students know that multiplication can be thought of as repeated addition, encourage them to write an addition sentence and a multiplication sentence for the improper fraction. They can write an addition sentence for the mixed number. Figure 6 shows $\frac{7}{6}$ and $1\frac{1}{6}$ with number sentences.

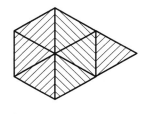

$$\frac{7}{6} = \frac{1}{6} + \frac{1}{6} + \frac{1}{6} + \frac{1}{6} + \frac{1}{6} + \frac{1}{6} + \frac{1}{6}$$
$$\frac{7}{6} = 7 \times \frac{1}{6}$$

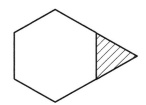

$$\frac{7}{6} = 1 + \frac{1}{6}$$
$$\frac{7}{6} = 1\frac{1}{6}$$

Figure 6: $\frac{7}{6}$ and $1\frac{1}{6}$ modeled with pattern blocks

Student Guide - page 75 *(Answers on p. 61)*

Student Guide - page 76 *(Answers on p. 62)*

Use the terms improper fraction and mixed number as you discuss the figures. An **improper fraction** is a fraction in which the numerator is greater than or equal to the denominator. A **mixed number** is made up of a whole number and a fraction. Be sure students understand that both the improper fraction and the mixed number in the illustration in the *Student Guide* represent the same quantity. They should also realize that improper fractions and mixed numbers always represent quantities greater than or equal to one. A **proper fraction** is a fraction less than one. The numerator is less than the denominator.

To complete **Questions 9–14,** students use pattern blocks to model fractions greater than one and then write number sentences for the models. As they work, ask students to look for strategies to help them write mixed numbers for improper fractions and improper fractions for mixed numbers when they do not have pattern blocks available. To guide their thinking ask,

- *Does the denominator change?*
- *What happens to the numerator?*
- *Use $\frac{11}{4}$ as an example. How many fourths make a whole?*

Questions 15–16 ask them to explain their strategies. In a class discussion, share student strategies. Help students develop meaningful and efficient procedures. Be sure they can clearly communicate their strategies in symbols and words. For example, to change $\frac{11}{4}$ to a mixed number, students can say: "I know the denominator stays the same. There are 4 fourths in one whole. I need to know how many wholes are in $\frac{11}{4}$. I think, 'How many groups of 4 fourths are in 11 fourths?' To find out, I divide 11 by 4. Since 11 divided by 4 is 2 with 3 left over, there are 2 wholes and 3 fourths left over." In symbols:

$$\frac{11}{4} = 11 \div 4 = 2\frac{3}{4}$$

To change $2\frac{3}{4}$ to an improper fraction, they can say: "There are 4 fourths in 1 whole, so there are 4×2 or 8 fourths in 2 wholes; 8 fourths plus the 3 fourths (from the fraction) is 11 fourths." In symbols:

$$2\frac{3}{4} = \frac{4 \times 2 + 3}{4} = \frac{11}{4}$$

TIMS Tip

While working on **Questions 9–14,** students may need to work in groups of four to have enough pattern blocks.

Math Facts

Use DPP items C and D to review the multiplication and division facts for the 2s and 3s and practice problem solving.

Homework and Practice

- Assign the problems in the Homework section of the *Student Guide.*

- Assign DPP Challenge D to practice problem solving.

- Assign Part 4 of the Home Practice.

Answers for Part 4 of the Home Practice are in the Answer Key at the end of this lesson and at the end of this unit.

Name _____ Date _____

PART 3 Fractions

1. Name a fraction between $\frac{1}{6}$ and 1. _____

2. Name a fraction between $\frac{1}{3}$ and 1. _____

3. Name a fraction with a denominator of 4 that is between 0 and 1. _____

4. Name a fraction greater than $\frac{1}{2}$ with a denominator of 8. _____

5. Name a fraction between $\frac{6}{8}$ and 1. _____

6. Which is greater:

    A. $\frac{1}{10}$ or $\frac{1}{12}$? _____

    B. $\frac{5}{8}$ or $\frac{3}{8}$? _____

    C. $\frac{7}{6}$ or 1? _____

    D. $\frac{1}{2}$ or $\frac{8}{10}$? _____

PART 4 Number Operations

1. Use paper and pencil to solve the following problems. Show your work on a separate sheet of paper. Estimate to make sure your answers are reasonable.

    A. $18 \times 36 =$ _____   B. $7430 + 578 =$ _____

    C. $8032 - 725 =$ _____   D. $623 \times 7 =$ _____

    E. $3419 + 7834 =$ _____   F. $2950 \times 5 =$ _____

2. Find the amount of change each person will receive in the following problems. For each, name the least number of coins and bills. Estimate to make sure your answers are reasonable.

    A. Manny buys a hamburger for $3.99, a baked potato for $1.79, and a drink for $1.29. He gives the salesclerk a $10 bill. How much change will he receive?

    B. Lin buys 3 gallons of bubble bath at $3.39 each. If Lin gives the salesclerk a $20 bill, how much change will she receive?

28 DAB • Grade 5 • Unit 3   FRACTIONS AND RATIOS

Discovery Assignment Book - page 28 *(Answers on p. 62)*

At a Glance

Math Facts and Daily Practice and Problems

Review the multiplication and division facts for the 2s and 3s. Complete DPP items C and D.

Part 1. Fraction Sentences

1. Students follow the example on the *Fraction Sentences* Activity Pages in the *Student Guide* by modeling one whole using three colors of pattern blocks. They write number sentences for their models.
2. Students work with partners to model fractions following specific criteria in *Questions 2–8.* Students write number sentences for their figures.
3. The class discusses *Question 7.* Students recognize that fractions with the same denominator and numerator equal one whole.

Part 2. Fractions Greater Than One

1. Using overhead pattern blocks, show the class a diagram of a mixed number and the equivalent improper fraction. Ask students to write number sentences for your figures. Discuss the terms improper fraction and mixed number.
2. In *Questions 9–14* in the *Student Guide,* students model improper fractions and mixed numbers using pattern blocks and write number sentences. As they work, they look for strategies for changing mixed numbers to improper fractions and improper fractions to mixed numbers. They may need to work in groups of four to have enough pattern blocks.
3. Students write their strategies and share them with the class *(Questions 15–16).* Help students use their strategies to develop meaningful and efficient procedures.
4. Students practice using the procedures in *Questions 17–18.*

Homework

1. Assign the Homework section in the *Student Guide.*
2. Assign Part 4 of the Home Practice.

Answer Key is on pages 59–62.

Notes:

Student Guide (p. 73)

Fraction Sentences

1. Answers will vary. One possible solution is: $\frac{5}{12} + \frac{1}{4} + \frac{1}{3} = 1$. See Figures 4 and 5 in Lesson Guide 2 for other solutions.*

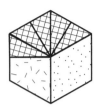

2. **A.** Answers will vary. Another possible number sentence is: $\frac{2}{6} + \frac{2}{12} = \frac{1}{2}$.

   B. Answers will vary. One possible solution is: $\frac{2}{12} + \frac{1}{3} = \frac{1}{2}$.

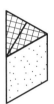

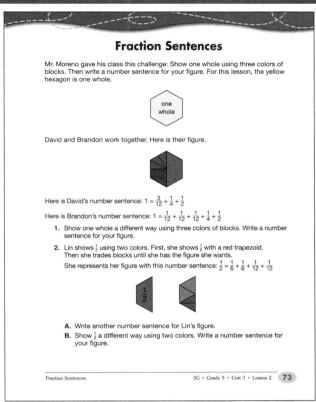

Fraction Sentences

Mr. Moreno gave his class this challenge: Show one whole using three colors of blocks. Then write a number sentence for your figure. For this lesson, the yellow hexagon is one whole.

one whole

David and Brandon work together. Here is their figure.

Here is David's number sentence: $1 = \frac{3}{12} + \frac{1}{4} + \frac{1}{2}$

Here is Brandon's number sentence: $1 = \frac{1}{12} + \frac{1}{12} + \frac{1}{12} + \frac{1}{4} + \frac{1}{2}$

1. Show one whole a different way using three colors of blocks. Write a number sentence for your figure.

2. Lin shows $\frac{1}{2}$ using two colors. First, she shows $\frac{1}{3}$ with a red trapezoid. Then she trades blocks until she has the figure she wants.

   She represents her figure with this number sentence: $\frac{1}{2} = \frac{1}{6} + \frac{1}{6} + \frac{1}{12} + \frac{1}{12}$

   A. Write another number sentence for Lin's figure.
   B. Show $\frac{1}{2}$ a different way using two colors. Write a number sentence for your figure.

Fraction Sentences   SG • Grade 5 • Unit 3 • Lesson 2   **73**

Student Guide - page 73

*Answers and/or discussion are included in the Lesson Guide.

For Questions 3–8, show the fraction. Then write a number sentence for your figure. Remember, the yellow hexagon is one whole.

3. Show $\frac{1}{2}$ using brown and two other colors.

4. Show $\frac{3}{4}$ using brown and two other colors. (*Hint:* Show $\frac{3}{4}$ with three browns first. Then, either cover the brown pieces or trade pieces.)

5. Show $\frac{5}{6}$ using purple, green, and blue.

6. Show $\frac{2}{3}$ without using blue.

7. **A.** Show one whole using one color. (Use any color but yellow.)
   B. Show one whole using a different color.
   C. What can you say about the numerator and denominator of a fraction that is equal to 1?

8. Show $\frac{5}{3}$ using two colors.

Fractions Greater Than One

Ana shows $\frac{5}{3}$ using one color and writes these number sentences:

$\frac{5}{3} = \frac{1}{3} + \frac{1}{3} + \frac{1}{3} + \frac{1}{3} + \frac{1}{3}$

$5 \times \frac{1}{3} = \frac{5}{3}$

When the numerator is greater than or equal to the denominator, the fraction is called an **improper fraction**. Both $\frac{5}{3}$ and $\frac{3}{3}$ are improper fractions. When the numerator is less than the denominator, such as $\frac{2}{3}$, the fraction is called a **proper fraction**.

Manny shows $\frac{5}{3}$ using yellow and blue and writes these number sentences:

$\frac{5}{3} = 1 + \frac{2}{3}$

$\frac{5}{3} = 1\frac{2}{3}$

Numbers that are made up of a whole number and a fraction are called **mixed numbers**. $1\frac{2}{3}$ is a mixed number.

74 SG • Grade 5 • Unit 3 • Lesson 2   Fraction Sentences

Student Guide - page 74

Student Guide (p. 74)

3. $\frac{1}{4} + \frac{1}{12} + \frac{1}{6} = \frac{1}{2}$

4. Answers will vary. One possible solution is:
$\frac{2}{4} + \frac{1}{12} + \frac{1}{6} = \frac{3}{4}$.

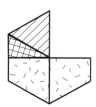

5. Answers will vary. One possible solution is:
$\frac{1}{3} + \frac{2}{6} + \frac{2}{12} = \frac{5}{6}$.

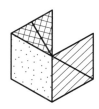

6. Answers will vary. One possible solution is:
$\frac{1}{6} + \frac{1}{6} + \frac{1}{6} + \frac{1}{6} = \frac{2}{3}$.

7.* **A.** Answers will vary. One possible solution is:
$\frac{1}{6} + \frac{1}{6} + \frac{1}{6} + \frac{1}{6} + \frac{1}{6} + \frac{1}{6} = 1$.

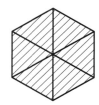

B. Answers will vary. One possible solution is:
$\frac{1}{3} + \frac{1}{3} + \frac{1}{3} = 1$.

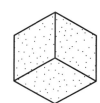

C. The numerator and denominator are the same number when the fraction is equal to 1.

8. Answers will vary. One possible solution is:
$\frac{1}{3} + \frac{1}{3} + \frac{1}{3} + \frac{1}{3} + \frac{1}{6} + \frac{1}{6} = \frac{5}{3}$.

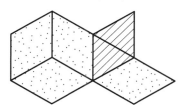

*Answers and/or discussion are included in the Lesson Guide.

Student Guide (p. 75)

9. A. Addition sentences will vary. One possible sentence is $\frac{1}{4} + \frac{1}{4} + \frac{1}{4} + \frac{1}{4} + \frac{1}{4} + \frac{1}{4} + \frac{1}{4} = \frac{7}{4}$; $7 \times \frac{1}{4} = \frac{7}{4}$.

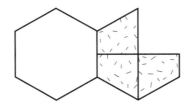

B. $1 + \frac{1}{4} + \frac{1}{4} + \frac{1}{4} = \frac{7}{4}$.

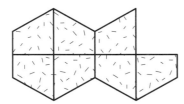

C. $1\frac{3}{4}$

10. A. Addition sentences will vary. One possible addition sentence is: $\frac{1}{2} + \frac{1}{2} + \frac{1}{2} + \frac{1}{2} + \frac{1}{2} = \frac{5}{2}$; $5 \times \frac{1}{2} = \frac{5}{2}$.

B. $1 + 1 + \frac{1}{2} = \frac{5}{2}$

C. $2\frac{1}{2}$

11. A. Answers will vary. One possible addition sentence is: $\frac{3}{3} + \frac{3}{3} + \frac{1}{3} = 2\frac{1}{3}$; $7 \times \frac{1}{3} = 2\frac{1}{3}$.

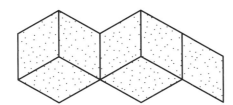

9. A. Show $\frac{7}{4}$ using only brown blocks. Write an addition sentence and a multiplication sentence for your figure.
  B. Show $\frac{7}{4}$ using yellow and brown blocks. Write an addition sentence for your figure.
  C. Write $\frac{7}{4}$ as a mixed number.
10. A. Show $\frac{5}{2}$ using only red blocks. Write an addition sentence and a multiplication sentence for your figure.
  B. Show $\frac{5}{2}$ using the fewest number of blocks possible. Write an addition sentence for your figure.
  C. Write a mixed number for $\frac{5}{2}$.
11. A. Show $2\frac{1}{3}$ using only blue blocks. Write a number sentence for your figure.
  B. Show $2\frac{1}{3}$ using the fewest number of blocks possible. Write an addition sentence for your figure.
  C. Write $2\frac{1}{3}$ as an improper fraction.
12. Write a mixed number and an improper fraction for the following figures:
  A.

  B.

13. Write each improper fraction as a mixed number. Use pattern blocks to help you.
  A. $\frac{9}{4}$ **B.** $\frac{17}{12}$ **C.** $\frac{11}{3}$ **D.** $\frac{11}{6}$
14. Write each mixed number as an improper fraction. You can use pattern blocks.
  A. $1\frac{1}{12}$ **B.** $3\frac{1}{2}$ **C.** $2\frac{2}{3}$ **D.** $2\frac{3}{4}$

Fraction Sentences   SG • Grade 5 • Unit 3 • Lesson 2   75

Student Guide - page 75

B. $1 + 1 + \frac{1}{3} = 2\frac{1}{3}$

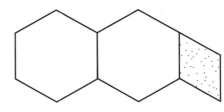

C. $\frac{7}{3}$

12. A. $3\frac{5}{6}$, $\frac{23}{6}$

  B. $3\frac{1}{2}$, $\frac{7}{2}$

13. A. $2\frac{1}{4}$

  B. $1\frac{5}{12}$

  C. $3\frac{2}{3}$

  D. $1\frac{5}{6}$

14. A. $\frac{13}{12}$

  B. $\frac{7}{2}$

  C. $\frac{8}{3}$

  D. $\frac{11}{4}$

15. Explain to a friend how you can change an improper fraction to a mixed number without using pattern blocks. Use an example in your explanation.

16. Explain to a friend how you can change a mixed number to an improper fraction without using pattern blocks. Use an example in your explanation.

17. Write each mixed number as an improper fraction.

    A. $1\frac{3}{8}$ B. $3\frac{3}{4}$ C. $3\frac{4}{5}$ D. $4\frac{5}{6}$

18. Write each improper fraction as a mixed number.

    A. $\frac{13}{4}$ B. $\frac{9}{2}$ C. $\frac{14}{3}$ D. $\frac{12}{5}$

Homework

1. Write a number sentence for each of the following figures. Remember, the yellow hexagon is one whole.

   A.   B.   C.   D.

2. Change each improper fraction to a mixed number.

   A. $\frac{11}{2}$ B. $\frac{19}{8}$ C. $\frac{19}{6}$ D. $\frac{19}{9}$

   E. $\frac{13}{5}$ F. $\frac{17}{3}$ G. $\frac{27}{4}$ H. $\frac{23}{10}$

3. Change each mixed number to an improper fraction.

   A. $4\frac{1}{6}$ B. $6\frac{1}{3}$

   C. $5\frac{3}{4}$ D. $3\frac{1}{10}$

   E. $6\frac{1}{2}$ F. $3\frac{4}{5}$

   G. $3\frac{3}{8}$ H. $1\frac{5}{9}$

Student Guide - page 76

Name _____ Date _____

PART 3 Fractions

1. Name a fraction between $\frac{1}{6}$ and 1. _____

2. Name a fraction between $\frac{1}{3}$ and 1. _____

3. Name a fraction with a denominator of 4 that is between 0 and 1. _____

4. Name a fraction greater than $\frac{1}{2}$ with a denominator of 8. _____

5. Name a fraction between $\frac{6}{8}$ and 1. _____

6. Which is greater:

   A. $\frac{1}{10}$ or $\frac{1}{12}$? _____

   B. $\frac{5}{8}$ or $\frac{3}{8}$? _____

   C. $\frac{7}{6}$ or 1? _____

   D. $\frac{1}{2}$ or $\frac{8}{10}$? _____

PART 4 Number Operations

1. Use paper and pencil to solve the following problems. Show your work on a separate sheet of paper. Estimate to make sure your answers are reasonable.

   A. $18 \times 36 =$ _____   B. $7430 + 578 =$ _____

   C. $8032 - 725 =$ _____   D. $623 \times 7 =$ _____

   E. $3419 + 7834 =$ _____   F. $2950 \times 5 =$ _____

2. Find the amount of change each person will receive in the following problems. For each, name the least number of coins and bills. Estimate to make sure your answers are reasonable.

   A. Manny buys a hamburger for $3.99, a baked potato for $1.79, and a drink for $1.29. He gives the salesclerk a $10 bill. How much change will he receive?

   B. Lin buys 3 gallons of bubble bath at $3.39 each. If Lin gives the salesclerk a $20 bill, how much change will she receive?

Discovery Assignment Book - page 28

Student Guide (p. 76)

15. Answers will vary.*

16. Answers will vary.*

17. A. $\frac{11}{8}$ B. $\frac{15}{4}$

    C. $\frac{19}{5}$ D. $\frac{29}{6}$

18. A. $3\frac{1}{4}$ B. $4\frac{1}{2}$

    C. $4\frac{2}{3}$ D. $2\frac{2}{5}$

Homework

1. A. Answers will vary. One possible solution is: $\frac{2}{6} + \frac{1}{3} + \frac{1}{4} + \frac{1}{12} = 1$.

   B. $\frac{1}{3} + \frac{1}{4} + \frac{1}{12} = \frac{2}{3}$

   C. Answers will vary. One possible solution is: $1 + \frac{3}{6} = 1\frac{3}{6}$ or $1\frac{1}{2}$.

   D. $\frac{1}{3} + \frac{1}{4} + \frac{1}{6} = \frac{3}{4}$

2. A. $5\frac{1}{2}$ B. $2\frac{3}{8}$

   C. $3\frac{1}{6}$ D. $2\frac{1}{9}$

   E. $2\frac{3}{5}$ F. $5\frac{2}{3}$

   G. $6\frac{3}{4}$ H. $2\frac{3}{10}$

3. A. $\frac{25}{6}$ B. $\frac{19}{3}$

   C. $\frac{23}{4}$ D. $\frac{31}{10}$

   E. $\frac{13}{2}$ F. $\frac{19}{5}$

   G. $\frac{27}{8}$ H. $\frac{14}{9}$

Discovery Assignment Book (p. 28)

Home Practice†

Part 4. Number Operations

1. A. 648

   B. 8008

   C. 7307

   D. 4361

   E. 11,253

   F. 14,750

2. A. $2.93; 2 dollars, 3 quarters, 1 dime, 1 nickel, 3 pennies

   B. $9.83; 9 dollars, 3 quarters, 1 nickel, 3 pennies

---

*Answers and/or discussion are included in the Lesson Guide.
†Answers for all the Home Practice in the *Discovery Assignment Book* are at the end of the unit.

Lesson 3

Equivalent Fractions

Key Content

- Representing fractions using pattern blocks and number lines.
- Finding equivalent fractions.

Key Vocabulary

- equivalent fractions

Math Facts

Review the multiplication and division facts for the 2s and 3s. Complete DPP item E.

Homework

Assign the homework in the *Student Guide.*

Assessment

1. Choose questions in the Homework section as assessment.
2. Use the journal prompt as an assessment.

Curriculum Sequence

Before This Unit

Students explored equivalent fractions using a paper folding model in third and fourth grades. In Grade 4 Unit 12 Lesson 5, students learned how to find fractions equivalent to a given fraction.

After This Unit

Students use equivalent fractions as they continue to study fractions, ratios, and proportions in Units 5, 11, 12, and 13.

Materials List

Supplies and Copies

Student	Teacher
Supplies for Each Student • ruler **Supplies for Each Student Pair** • 1 set of pattern blocks (2–3 yellow hexagons, 6 red trapezoids, 10 blue rhombuses, 10 green triangles, 6 brown trapezoids, 12 purple triangles)	**Supplies** • colored chalk, optional • overhead pattern blocks, optional
Copies	**Copies/Transparencies** • 1 transparency of *Number Lines for Fractohoppers,* optional (*Discovery Assignment Book* Page 39)

All blackline masters including assessment, transparency, and DPP masters are also on the Teacher Resource CD.

Student Books

Equivalent Fractions (*Student Guide* Pages 77–81)
Number Lines for Fractohoppers (*Discovery Assignment Book* Page 39)

Daily Practice and Problems and Home Practice

DPP items E–H (*Unit Resource Guide* Pages 18–20)

Note: Classrooms whose pacing differs significantly from the suggested pacing of the units should use the Math Facts Calendar in Section 4 of the *Facts Resource Guide* to ensure students receive the complete math facts program.

Daily Practice and Problems

Suggestions for using the DPPs are on page 70.

E. Bit: Fact Families for × and ÷
(URG p. 18)

Solve each pair of related facts. Then name two other facts in the same fact family.

A. $4 \times 2 = ?$ and $8 \div 2 = ?$

B. $9 \times 3 = ?$ and $27 \div 3 = ?$

C. $3 \times 5 = ?$ and $15 \div 3 = ?$

D. $2 \times 8 = ?$ and $16 \div 8 = ?$

E. $10 \times 2 = ?$ and $20 \div 10 = ?$

F. $4 \times 3 = ?$ and $12 \div 3 = ?$

G. $7 \times 2 = ?$ and $14 \div 2 = ?$

H. $3 \times 6 = ?$ and $18 \div 3 = ?$

F. Task: Finding the Median
(URG p. 19)

Use the data in the graph to answer the questions.

1. What is the most common number of pets? (What is the mode?)

2. How many students were surveyed in Room 306?

3. Use the graph to find the median number of pets owned by students in Room 306.

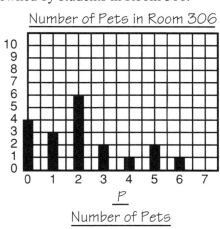

G. Bit: Arithmetic Review
(URG p. 19)

Use paper and pencil to solve these problems. Estimate to see if your answers are reasonable.

A. 54×8

B. $534 + 963$

C. 730×6

D. $5001 - 3989$

H. Task: Parts of a Whole (URG p. 20)

You may use pattern blocks to help you with these problems.

1. If this is $\frac{1}{2}$,

draw 1 whole.

2. If this is one whole,

A. Show $\frac{2}{3}$.   B. Show $\frac{4}{3}$.

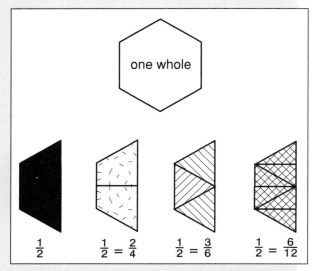

Figure 7: *Fractions equivalent to $\frac{1}{2}$ modeled with pattern blocks*

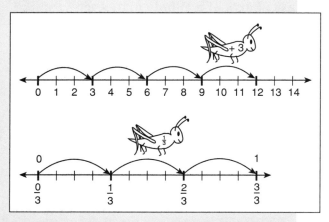

Figure 8: *A +3 mathhopper and $\frac{1}{3}$ hopper*

Teaching the Activity

Part 1 Equivalent Fractions and Pattern Blocks

To begin this lesson, students model equivalent fractions as shown at the beginning of the *Equivalent Fractions* Activity Pages in the *Student Guide*. *Questions 1–2* ask students to show equivalent fractions with pattern blocks and write number sentences for each pair of equivalent fractions. *Question 2E* asks for all the fractions equivalent to $\frac{1}{2}$ that students can show with pattern blocks. These fractions are shown in Figure 7. (The yellow hexagon is one whole.)

Use *Question 3* to guide a class discussion of the patterns students find in their number sentences for *Question 2E*. They can say the numerator is half the denominator or the denominator is twice the numerator. Also, multiplying the numerator and denominator by the same number will result in a fraction equivalent to $\frac{1}{2}$.

Part 2 Equivalent Fractions and Fractohoppers

Students continue to explore fractions using number lines. In earlier grades, children worked with mathhoppers. Mathhoppers are imaginary creatures that hop along the number line. A +3 mathhopper jumps 3 units at a time, by multiples of 3. See Figure 8.

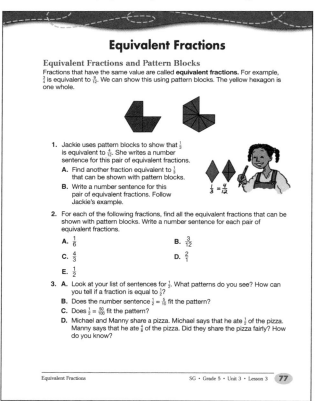

Equivalent Fractions

Equivalent Fractions and Pattern Blocks
Fractions that have the same value are called **equivalent fractions.** For example, $\frac{3}{4}$ is equivalent to $\frac{9}{12}$. We can show this using pattern blocks. The yellow hexagon is one whole.

1. Jackie uses pattern blocks to show that $\frac{1}{3}$ is equivalent to $\frac{4}{12}$. She writes a number sentence for this pair of equivalent fractions.
    A. Find another fraction equivalent to $\frac{1}{3}$ that can be shown with pattern blocks.
    B. Write a number sentence for this pair of equivalent fractions. Follow Jackie's example.

2. For each of the following fractions, find all the equivalent fractions that can be shown with pattern blocks. Write a number sentence for each pair of equivalent fractions.
    A. $\frac{1}{6}$ B. $\frac{3}{12}$
    C. $\frac{4}{3}$ D. $\frac{2}{1}$
    E. $\frac{1}{2}$

3. A. Look at your list of sentences for $\frac{1}{2}$. What patterns do you see? How can you tell if a fraction is equal to $\frac{1}{2}$?
    B. Does the number sentence $\frac{1}{2} = \frac{5}{10}$ fit the pattern?
    C. Does $\frac{1}{2} = \frac{50}{100}$ fit the pattern?
    D. Michael and Manny share a pizza. Michael says that he ate $\frac{1}{2}$ of the pizza. Manny says that he ate $\frac{4}{8}$ of the pizza. Did they share the pizza fairly? How do you know?

Equivalent Fractions   SG • Grade 5 • Unit 3 • Lesson 3   **77**

Student Guide - page 77 *(Answers on p. 72)*

We now introduce fractohoppers. Fractohoppers are the same as mathhoppers, but they jump fractional amounts. A $\frac{1}{3}$ fractohopper jumps by one-third units as shown in Figure 8.

Sketch a number line on the board or overhead as shown in Figure 9. A $\frac{1}{4}$ fractohopper can jump on this line.

Use the following discussion prompts:

- *Where will the $\frac{1}{4}$ hopper land if it starts at zero and jumps three times?* ($\frac{3}{4}$)

- *Where is the $\frac{1}{4}$ hopper if it starts at zero and takes no jumps?* (0 which can be written as $\frac{0}{4}$)

- *Where will the $\frac{1}{4}$ hopper land if it starts at zero and hops 4 times?* ($\frac{4}{4}$ or 1)

- *Can any other fractohoppers jump on this line? Which one?* ($\frac{1}{2}$ hopper; Show the 2 jumps a $\frac{1}{2}$ hopper makes on the number line.)

- *Where does the $\frac{1}{2}$ hopper land if it hops one time?* ($\frac{2}{4}$ or $\frac{1}{2}$; Write $\frac{1}{2}$ above $\frac{2}{4}$ on the number line.)

Note to students that if the $\frac{1}{4}$ hopper jumps 2 times, it lands in the same place as the $\frac{1}{2}$ hopper jumping once. This is another way of observing that $\frac{2}{4} = \frac{1}{2}$. If available, use different-colored chalk (or overhead pens) to illustrate the different jumps. It is important to note that while there is a distinction between a $\frac{1}{4}$ hopper jumping two times and a $\frac{1}{2}$ hopper jumping once, they end up in the same place. Mathematically we are saying:

$$1 \times \tfrac{1}{2} = 1 \times \tfrac{2}{4} = 2 \times \tfrac{1}{4} = \tfrac{1}{4} + \tfrac{1}{4} = \tfrac{1}{2}$$

You may want to sketch a number line for a $\frac{1}{8}$ hopper on the board or overhead and ask similar questions about $\frac{1}{8}$ hoppers, $\frac{1}{4}$ hoppers, and $\frac{1}{2}$ hoppers using this number line. Include questions that ask about the fractohoppers landing at 0 and 1.

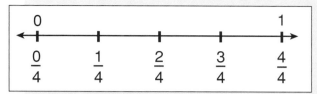

Figure 9: *A number line for a $\frac{1}{4}$ hopper*

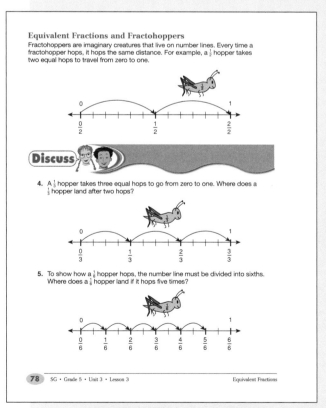

Equivalent Fractions and Fractohoppers

Fractohoppers are imaginary creatures that live on number lines. Every time a fractohopper hops, it hops the same distance. For example, a $\frac{1}{2}$ hopper takes two equal hops to travel from zero to one.

Discuss

4. A $\frac{1}{3}$ hopper takes three equal hops to go from zero to one. Where does a $\frac{1}{3}$ hopper land after two hops?

5. To show how a $\frac{1}{6}$ hopper hops, the number line must be divided into sixths. Where does a $\frac{1}{6}$ hopper land if it hops five times?

78   SG • Grade 5 • Unit 3 • Lesson 3   Equivalent Fractions

Student Guide - page 78 (Answers on p. 72)

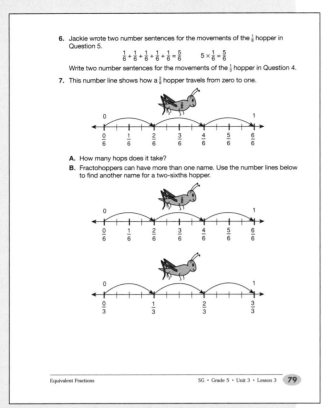

Student Guide - page 79 *(Answers on p. 73)*

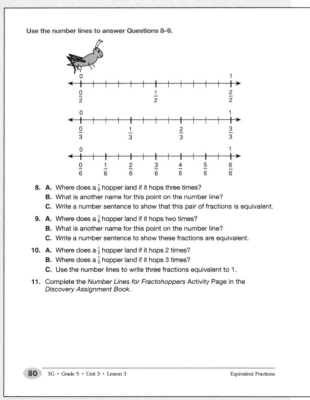

Student Guide - page 80 *(Answers on p. 73)*

With this introduction, students can complete *Questions 4–10* in the Equivalent Fractions and Fractohoppers section of the *Student Guide*. In *Question 6,* students are reminded that a multiplication sentence can represent a repeated addition sentence. So two sentences for the movements of the $\frac{1}{3}$ hopper in *Question 4* are $\frac{1}{3} + \frac{1}{3} = \frac{2}{3}$ and $2 \times \frac{1}{3} = \frac{2}{3}$.

Part 3 **Using Number Lines to Find Equivalent Fractions**

Question 11 in the *Student Guide* asks students to complete the *Number Lines for Fractohoppers* Activity Page in the *Discovery Assignment Book*. When completed, this page provides students with a visual record of fraction equivalencies. They will use this page as a reference in future work with fractions.

Discuss strategies for completing the number lines. Students will need a pencil and a ruler to work on this page. Note that the lines for halves, thirds, fourths, sixths, and twelfths are divided into twelfths. Students should make larger tick marks for each fraction they are to label, as shown on the number line for thirds. Each number line is ten centimeters long, so students can make tick marks for fifths (2 cm apart) and tenths (1 cm apart) using a centimeter ruler. They can complete the number line for eighths by using the ruler to divide the number line in half, then dividing the halves into fourths, then dividing the fourths into eighths. If necessary, use a transparency of the *Number Lines for Fractohoppers* Activity Page to demonstrate specific strategies.

Since students will use these number lines to find equivalent fractions in this lesson, it is important that students complete the page accurately. Check to see that the divisions of the lines are accurate and that students label them correctly. They can check their work by turning to the completed Number Lines for Fractohoppers chart in the *Student Guide* for Lesson 4.

Students use their completed copy of the *Number Lines for Fractohoppers* Activity Page to answer *Questions 12–17.* They use the number lines to find equivalent fractions. *Questions 13–16* explore specific procedures for writing pairs of equivalent fractions. *Question 13* asks students to list all the fractions on the number lines equivalent to $\frac{3}{4}$. Then they look for patterns in the number sentences they write. A pattern similar to one described in *Question 3* can be restated. Multiplying the numerator and denominator of $\frac{3}{4}$ by the same number will give an equivalent fraction. *Question 14* makes this explicit:

$$\frac{3}{4} = \frac{3 \times 2}{4 \times 2} = \frac{6}{8} \text{ and } \frac{3}{4} = \frac{3 \times 3}{4 \times 3} = \frac{9}{12}$$

Questions 15–16 discuss dividing the numerator and denominator of a fraction by the same number to find an equivalent fraction.

Discuss **Question 17** as a group. Students list all the fractions on the number lines equivalent to 1. Make sure students realize that three jumps of the $\frac{1}{3}$ hopper is the same as a $+1$ mathhopper jumping once. In other words, $\frac{3}{3} = 1$. Ask, *"How can you tell if a fraction is equal to 1? Is $\frac{98,765}{98,765}$ equivalent to 1?"*

Question 18 asks students to explain a method for finding equivalent fractions. Help students articulate in words the patterns they have observed using pattern blocks, number lines, and number sentences. Students might say: "Multiply or divide the numerator and denominator of a fraction by the same number to find an equivalent fraction." Encourage students to use symbols to give examples as in **Questions 14** and **16**. **Question 19** asks students to apply their method.

Content Note

The idea that $\frac{3}{3}$, $\frac{4}{4}$, $\frac{5}{5}$, etc., all are equivalent to 1 needs to be revisited often. This will help prepare children for later work with fractions.

Note that multiplying the numerator and denominator of a fraction by the same number is equivalent to multiplying by one. Since $\frac{2}{2} = 1$,

$$\frac{3}{4} \times 1 = \frac{3}{4} \times \frac{2}{2}$$
$$\frac{3}{4} = \frac{6}{8}$$

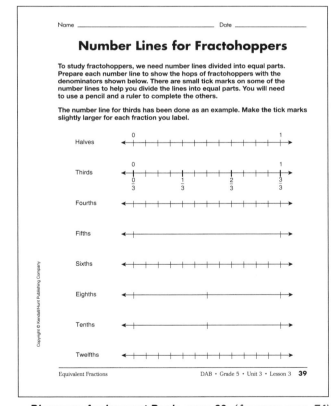

Discovery Assignment Book - page 39 (Answers on p. 74)

Student Guide - page 81 (Answers on p. 74)

Math Facts

Use Daily Practice and Problems item E to complete fact families for the 2s and 3s.

Homework and Practice

- Assign the Homework section in the *Student Guide.*
- Remind students to use their triangle flash cards to review the math facts for the 2s and 3s at home.
- Use DPP items F, G, and H to review medians, computation, and parts of a whole.

Assessment

- Use the questions in the homework as an assessment.
- Use student responses to the journal prompt to assess their understanding of equivalent fractions. Can students apply the procedures they developed in class for finding equivalent fractions? Can they explain their reasoning?

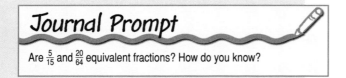

Journal Prompt

Are $\frac{5}{15}$ and $\frac{20}{64}$ equivalent fractions? How do you know?

At a Glance

Math Facts and Daily Practice and Problems

Review the multiplication and division facts for the 2s and 3s. Complete DPP items E–H.

Part 1. Equivalent Fractions and Pattern Blocks

1. Students use pattern blocks to model equivalent fractions. They write number sentences showing pairs of equivalent fractions. *(Questions 1–2)*
2. Students describe patterns in their list of number sentences for $\frac{1}{2}$. *(Question 3)*

Part 2. Equivalent Fractions and Fractohoppers

1. Introduce fractohoppers using a number line for a $\frac{1}{4}$ hopper and the discussion prompts in the Lesson Guide. Repeat for a $\frac{1}{8}$ hopper.
2. Discuss equivalent fractions on the number line using *Questions 4–10* in the Equivalent Fractions and Fractohoppers section in the *Student Guide.*
3. Students complete the *Number Lines for Fractohoppers* Activity Page in the *Discovery Assignment Book.* (*Question 11* in the *Student Guide*)

Part 3. Using Number Lines to Find Equivalent Fractions

1. Students use their number lines to answer *Questions 12–17* in the Using Number Lines to Find Equivalent Fractions section of the *Student Guide.*
2. Students describe methods for finding equivalent fractions. *(Question 18)*
3. Students apply their methods in *Question 19.*

Homework

Assign the homework in the *Student Guide.*

Assessment

1. Choose questions in the Homework section as assessment.
2. Use the journal prompt as an assessment.

Answer Key is on pages 72–74.

Notes:

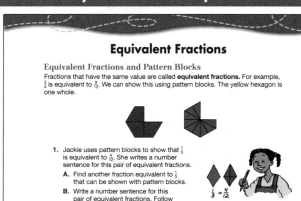

Student Guide - page 77

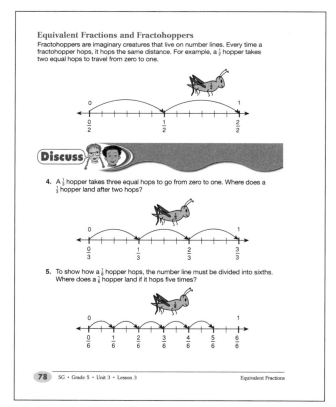

Student Guide - page 78

*Answers and/or discussion are included in the Lesson Guide.

Student Guide (p. 77)

Equivalent Fractions

1. **A.** Answers will vary. One possible solution is shown. $\frac{2}{6}$

B. $\frac{1}{3} = \frac{2}{6}$

2. **A.** $\frac{1}{6} = \frac{2}{12}$

B. $\frac{3}{12} = \frac{1}{4}$

C. $\frac{4}{3} = \frac{8}{6}, \frac{4}{3} = \frac{16}{12}$

D. $\frac{2}{1} = \frac{4}{2}$ $\frac{2}{1} = \frac{6}{3}$ $\frac{2}{1} = \frac{8}{4}$ $\frac{2}{1} = \frac{12}{6}$ $\frac{2}{1} = \frac{24}{12}$

E. See Figure 7 in Lesson Guide 3 for pictures of pattern block fractions.*

$$\frac{1}{2} = \frac{2}{4}$$
$$\frac{1}{2} = \frac{3}{6}$$
$$\frac{1}{2} = \frac{6}{12}$$

3. **A.** Answers will vary. The denominator is twice the numerator. If you multiply the numerator by 2, you will get the denominator. The numerator is half the denominator. All the denominators are even numbers. Multiplying numerator and denominator by the same number results in a fraction equivalent to $\frac{1}{2}$.*

B. Yes

C. Yes

D. Yes. $\frac{1}{2} = \frac{4}{8}$

Student Guide (p. 78)

4. $\frac{2}{3}$

5. $\frac{5}{6}$

Student Guide (p. 79)

6.* $\frac{1}{3} + \frac{1}{3} = \frac{2}{3}$ and $2 \times \frac{1}{3} = \frac{2}{3}$

7. A. 3 hops

 B. $\frac{1}{3}$ hopper

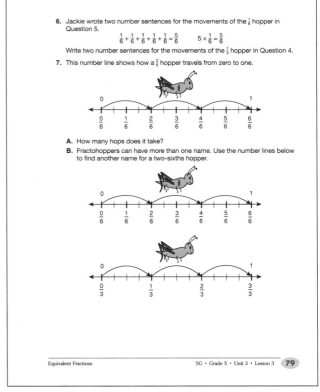

Student Guide - page 79

Student Guide (p. 80)

8. A. $\frac{3}{6}$

 B. $\frac{1}{2}$

 C. $\frac{1}{2} = \frac{3}{6}$

9. A. $\frac{2}{6}$

 B. $\frac{1}{3}$

 C. $\frac{1}{3} = \frac{2}{6}$

10. A. 1

 B. 1

 C. $\frac{2}{2}, \frac{3}{3}, \frac{6}{6}$

11. See the Number Lines for Fractohoppers chart on the first page of the *Comparing Fractions* Activity Pages in the Student Guide for Lesson 4.

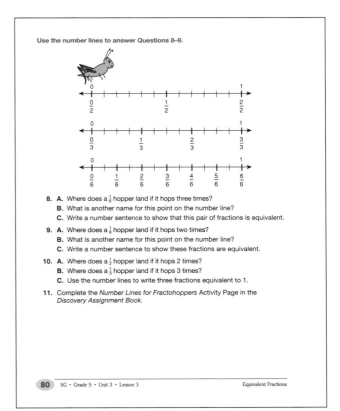

Student Guide - page 80

*Answers and/or discussion are included in the Lesson Guide.

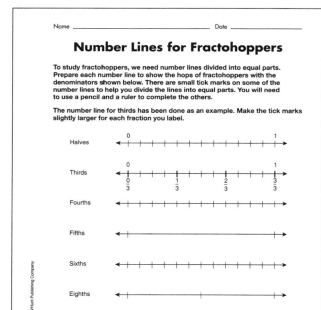

Student Guide - page 81

Discovery Assignment Book - page 39

*Answers and/or discussion are included in the Lesson Guide.

Student Guide (p. 81)

12. **A.** $\frac{2}{5} = \frac{4}{10}$ **B.** $\frac{10}{12} = \frac{5}{6}$

 C. $\frac{1}{4} = \frac{3}{12}$ **D.** $\frac{1}{4} = \frac{2}{8}$

 E. $\frac{8}{10} = \frac{4}{5}$ **F.** $\frac{1}{3} = \frac{4}{12}$

13. **A.** $\frac{3}{4} = \frac{6}{8}; \frac{3}{4} = \frac{9}{12}$

 B. The numerators are all multiples of 3. The denominators are multiples of 4. If you multiply the numerator and denominator by the same number you will get a fraction equivalent to $\frac{3}{4}$.*

14.* Yes; $\frac{3 \times 5}{4 \times 5} = \frac{15}{20}$

15. **A.** $\frac{8}{12} = \frac{4}{6}; \frac{8}{12} = \frac{2}{3}$

 B. The numerators are multiples of 2. The denominators are multiples of 3. If you divide 8 and 12 by the same number you get a fraction equivalent to $\frac{8}{12}$.

16. Yes. They name the same point on the number line. $\frac{8 \div 2}{12 \div 2} = \frac{4}{6}$

17.* $\frac{2}{3}, \frac{3}{4}, \frac{4}{5}, \frac{5}{6}, \frac{6}{8}, \frac{8}{10}, \frac{10}{12}, \frac{12}{12}$

18. If you multiply or divide the numerator and denominator by the same number you will get an equivalent fraction.*

19. **A.** $\frac{1}{4} = \frac{5}{20}$ **B.** $\frac{2}{5} = \frac{8}{20}$

 C. $\frac{4}{3} = \frac{12}{9}$ **D.** $\frac{8}{16} = \frac{2}{4}$

 E. $\frac{3}{15} = \frac{1}{5}$ **F.** $\frac{1}{4} = \frac{25}{100}$

Homework

 A. $\frac{8}{10} = \frac{4}{5}$ **B.** $\frac{8}{3} = \frac{16}{6}$

 C. $\frac{75}{100} = \frac{3}{4}$ **D.** $\frac{5}{8} = \frac{10}{16}$

 E. $\frac{10}{3} = \frac{30}{9}$ **F.** $\frac{30}{50} = \frac{3}{5}$

 G. $\frac{7}{3} = \frac{28}{12}$ **H.** $\frac{2}{5} = \frac{8}{20}$

 I. $\frac{6}{9} = \frac{2}{3}$

Discovery Assignment Book (p. 39)

Number Lines for Fractohoppers

See the Number Lines for Fractohoppers chart on the first page of the *Comparing Fractions* Activity Pages in the *Student Guide* (Lesson 4) for complete number lines.

Lesson 4

Comparing Fractions

Lesson Overview

Estimated Class Sessions

1

Students compare and order fractions using the benchmarks of 0, $\frac{1}{2}$, 1, and more than 1. Students order sets of fractions with common denominators and sets of fractions with common numerators. Number lines provide a visual model for students as they order fractions according to size.

Key Content

- Comparing and ordering fractions using benchmarks.
- Comparing and ordering fractions with common denominators.
- Comparing and ordering fractions with common numerators.

Key Vocabulary

- benchmarks

Math Facts

Review the multiplication and division facts for the 2s and 3s. Complete DPP item I.

Homework

1. Assign Homework *Questions 1–6* in the *Student Guide*.
2. Assign Part 3 of the Home Practice.

Assessment

Use Part 6 of the Home Practice as an assessment.

Curriculum Sequence

Before This Unit

Students compared and ordered fractions in third and fourth grade. In Grade 4 Unit 12 students used a paper folding model to compare fractions in Lessons 1 and 3. They played a game to practice comparing fractions in Lesson 4.

After This Unit

Students will continue to order and compare fractions using different tools in later units. In Unit 5 they will use rectangles on paper to model using common denominators to compare fractions. In Unit 11 they compare fractions by finding common denominators using multiples.

Materials List

Supplies and Copies

Student	Teacher
Supplies for Each Student Pair • pattern blocks, optional	**Supplies**
Copies	**Copies/Transparencies** • 1 transparency of *Number Lines for Fractohoppers* chart (*Student Guide* Page 82)

All blackline masters including assessment, transparency, and DPP masters are also on the Teacher Resource CD.

Student Books

Comparing Fractions (*Student Guide* Pages 82–84)
Completed *Number Lines for Fractohopppers* (*Discovery Assignment Book* Page 39), optional

Daily Practice and Problems and Home Practice

DPP items I–J (*Unit Resource Guide* Pages 20–21)
Home Practice Parts 3 & 6 (*Discovery Assignment Book* Pages 28 and 30)

Note: Classrooms whose pacing differs significantly from the suggested pacing of the units should use the Math Facts Calendar in Section 4 of the *Facts Resource Guide* to ensure students receive the complete math facts program.

Daily Practice and Problems

Suggestions for using the DPPs are on page 80.

I. Bit: Mixed Numbers and
Improper Fractions (URG p. 20)

1. Write a whole number or a mixed number for each improper fraction.

   A. $\frac{15}{4}$ B. $\frac{24}{8}$ C. $\frac{29}{3}$

2. Write an improper fraction for each mixed number.

   A. $6\frac{2}{3}$ B. $9\frac{1}{2}$ C. $5\frac{1}{3}$

J. Task: Fraction Skip Counting
   (URG p. 21)

Work with a partner on these problems. Take turns timing each other.

1. Skip count by halves for 15 seconds. Write down how far you were able to count. Start like this: $\frac{1}{2}$, 1, $1\frac{1}{2}$, 2, $2\frac{1}{2}$, 3 . . .

2. Skip count by thirds for 15 seconds. Write down how far you were able to count.

3. Estimate how far you think you can count by fifths in 15 seconds. Try it. How close was your estimate?

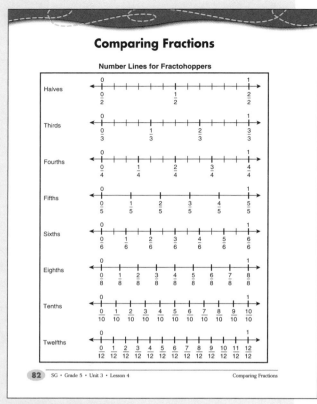

Student Guide - page 82

Student Guide - page 83 *(Answers on p. 82)*

Review the *Number Lines for Fractohoppers* Activity Page from Lesson 3 with students. A completed chart of the number lines is provided on the first page of the *Comparing Fractions* Activity Pages in the *Student Guide*. Identify 0, $\frac{1}{2}$, and 1 as benchmarks on these number lines. Ask students how they might use these benchmarks to compare the size of fractions. Then have students turn to the table at the top of the second page and look for patterns. Students can work in small groups to discuss patterns they see.

Ask students to draw a four-column table like the one in the *Student Guide*. After students draw the table, have them complete **Question 1.** Encourage students to use the number lines to help them as needed. After they add the fractions in **Question 1** to the table, students can compare their tables with a partner's and discuss any differences.

In **Question 2,** students describe the similarities of fractions that are close to each benchmark. They discuss these questions in pairs or small groups. Then they share their ideas with the whole class. Their responses may include:

*   Fractions equal to zero have zero for a numerator.

*   Fractions near zero have small numerators but much larger denominators.

*   Fractions near $\frac{1}{2}$ have numerators that are about half of the denominators.

*   Fractions equal to $\frac{1}{2}$ have numerators that are exactly half of the denominators. The denominators are twice the numerators.

*   Fractions equal to 1 have the same numerator and denominator.

*   Fractions close to 1 have numerators that are almost the same as the denominators.

*   Fractions much greater than one have numerators that are much larger than the denominators.

Division by Zero. Division by zero is undefined. Therefore, fractions equal to zero will have a zero in the numerator, but not in the denominator.

Questions 3–4 ask students to add fractions to their tables. After providing time to complete each question, allow students to share their answers and strategies. Answer any questions about using benchmarks when comparing fractions.

Students order sets of fractions from smallest to largest in *Question 5.* Encourage students to think about strategies they can use to complete this task. One way to do this is to have students work in pairs. Have each partner try a different strategy to order the fractions and then compare results. For example, one partner can use benchmarks and the other, number lines.

In *Questions 6–7,* students use benchmarks or number lines to order two sets of fractions from smallest to largest. Remind students that they may also use pattern blocks. The fractions in *Question 6* have common denominators; those in *Question 7* have common numerators. Students should look for patterns in the ordered fractions. They can see that if a set of fractions has common denominators, the set can be ordered using the numerators. Students should see that when the denominators are the same, the smaller the numerator, the smaller the fraction.

Therefore: $\frac{1}{5} < \frac{3}{5} < \frac{4}{5} < \frac{6}{5}$.

If a set of fractions has a common numerator, the set can be ordered using the denominators. When numerators are the same, the smaller the denominator, the larger the fraction.

Therefore: $\frac{1}{12} < \frac{1}{10} < \frac{1}{4} < \frac{1}{3} < \frac{1}{2}$.

Question 8 provides additional practice in ordering fractions.

7. Write each of the following sets of fractions in order from smallest to largest.
   A. $\frac{1}{3}, \frac{1}{4}, \frac{1}{2}, \frac{1}{10}$
   B. $\frac{3}{5}, \frac{3}{10}, \frac{3}{8}, \frac{3}{2}$
   C. If two or more fractions have the same numerator, how can you tell which of the fractions is larger?

8. Write each of the following sets of fractions in order from smallest to largest.
   A. $\frac{7}{12}, \frac{3}{8}, \frac{1}{12}, \frac{10}{10}$ B. $\frac{2}{9}, \frac{12}{11}, \frac{8}{14}, \frac{4}{8}$
   C. $\frac{7}{8}, \frac{7}{4}, \frac{7}{11}, \frac{7}{9}$ D. $\frac{9}{6}, \frac{3}{6}, \frac{1}{6}, \frac{5}{6}$
   E. $\frac{2}{12}, \frac{20}{10}, \frac{4}{6}, \frac{2}{4}$ F. $\frac{7}{10}, \frac{10}{9}, \frac{1}{10}, \frac{4}{9}$

 **Homework**

Write the following sets of fractions in order from smallest to largest. Use the strategies that you have learned. Tell which strategy you used to answer each question.

1. $\frac{2}{12}, \frac{2}{3}, \frac{2}{5}, \frac{2}{10}$
2. $\frac{7}{8}, \frac{1}{12}, \frac{3}{6}, \frac{13}{5}$
3. $\frac{3}{10}, \frac{7}{10}, \frac{2}{10}, \frac{5}{10}$
4. $\frac{11}{12}, \frac{4}{9}, \frac{0}{3}, \frac{1}{3}$
5. $\frac{5}{9}, \frac{5}{4}, \frac{5}{12}, \frac{5}{6}$
6. Manny walks $\frac{1}{3}$ mile to school each day. David walks $\frac{2}{3}$ mile to school, and Brandon walks $\frac{1}{4}$ mile.
   A. Who has the shortest walk? Explain how you know.
   B. Who has the longest walk? Explain how you know.

Student Guide - page 84   (Answers on p. 83)

Name _____ Date _____

PART 3 Fractions

1. Name a fraction between $\frac{1}{6}$ and 1. _____

2. Name a fraction between $\frac{1}{3}$ and 1. _____

3. Name a fraction with a denominator of 4 that is between 0 and 1. _____

4. Name a fraction greater than $\frac{1}{2}$ with a denominator of 8. _____

5. Name a fraction between $\frac{6}{8}$ and 1. _____

6. Which is greater:

   A. $\frac{1}{10}$ or $\frac{1}{12}$? _____

   B. $\frac{5}{8}$ or $\frac{3}{8}$? _____

   C. $\frac{7}{6}$ or 1? _____

   D. $\frac{1}{2}$ or $\frac{8}{10}$? _____

PART 4 Number Operations

1. Use paper and pencil to solve the following problems. Show your work on a separate sheet of paper. Estimate to make sure your answers are reasonable.

   A. $18 \times 36 =$ _____   B. $7430 + 578 =$ _____

   C. $8032 - 725 =$ _____   D. $623 \times 7 =$ _____

   E. $3419 + 7834 =$ _____   F. $2950 \times 5 =$ _____

2. Find the amount of change each person will receive in the following problems. For each, name the least number of coins and bills. Estimate to make sure your answers are reasonable.

   A. Manny buys a hamburger for $3.99, a baked potato for $1.79, and a drink for $1.29. He gives the salesclerk a $10 bill. How much change will he receive?

   B. Lin buys 3 gallons of bubble bath at $3.39 each. If Lin gives the salesclerk a $20 bill, how much change will she receive?

28 DAB • Grade 5 • Unit 3   FRACTIONS AND RATIOS

Discovery Assignment Book - page 28 (Answers on p. 83)

Math Facts

Assign Bit I. Students use the multiplication and division facts for the 2s and 3s to write improper fractions as mixed numbers.

Homework and Practice

- Assign Homework *Questions 1–6* on the *Comparing Fractions* Activity Pages in the *Student Guide*.

- Assign DPP item J to practice skip counting with fractions.

- Assign Part 3 of the Home Practice for homework.

Answers for Parts 3 and 6 of the Home Practice are in the Answer Key at the end of this lesson and at the end of this unit.

Assessment

Use Part 6 of the Home Practice as an assessment of students' skills with ordering fractions, finding equivalent fractions, converting mixed numbers to improper fractions, and converting improper fractions to mixed numbers.

Name _____ Date _____

PART 6 A Fraction More

1. Complete the following number sentences. The Number Lines for Fractohoppers chart you completed in Lesson 3 or the chart in Lesson 4 of the *Student Guide* may help you solve some of the problems.

   A. $\frac{1}{3} = \frac{2}{n}$ B. $\frac{9}{12} = \frac{n}{4}$ C. $\frac{2}{6} = \frac{n}{12}$

   D. $\frac{5}{8} = \frac{15}{n}$ E. $\frac{20}{70} = \frac{n}{7}$ F. $\frac{7}{9} = \frac{n}{36}$

   G. $\frac{3}{5} = \frac{n}{25}$ H. $\frac{4}{40} = \frac{1}{n}$ I. $\frac{2}{3} = \frac{8}{n}$

2. Write each mixed number as an improper fraction.

   A. $1\frac{1}{4}$ B. $5\frac{2}{3}$ C. $2\frac{7}{8}$ D. $3\frac{3}{5}$

3. Write each improper fraction as a mixed number.

   A. $\frac{9}{4}$ B. $\frac{20}{6}$ C. $\frac{21}{2}$ D. $\frac{23}{12}$

4. Put each of the following sets of fractions in order from smallest to largest.

   A. $\frac{9}{5}, \frac{9}{10}, \frac{9}{2}, \frac{9}{12}$ B. $\frac{5}{6}, \frac{8}{7}, \frac{7}{12}, \frac{1}{8}$

   C. $\frac{6}{6}, \frac{3}{6}, \frac{10}{6}, \frac{2}{6}$ D. $\frac{3}{20}, \frac{3}{2}, \frac{9}{11}, \frac{9}{16}$

30 DAB • Grade 5 • Unit 3   FRACTIONS AND RATIOS

Discovery Assignment Book - page 30 (Answers on p. 84)

Estimated Class Sessions

1

At a Glance

Math Facts and Daily Practice and Problems

Review the multiplication and division facts for the 2s and 3s. Complete DPP items I–J.

Teaching the Activity

1. Review the *Number Lines for Fractohoppers* Activity Pages from Lesson 3. A completed chart is on the first page of the *Comparing Fractions* Activity Pages in the *Student Guide.*
2. Identify 0, $\frac{1}{2}$, and 1 as benchmarks for comparing fractions. Students discuss patterns they see in the table on the second page of the *Comparing Fractions* Activity Pages. Students make a table as shown in the *Student Guide* and add fractions to the table. *(Questions 1–4)*
3. They sort fractions by size using the benchmarks table or the Number Lines for Fractohoppers chart. *(Question 5)*
4. Students order fractions from smallest to largest using common denominators. *(Question 6)*
5. Students order fractions from smallest to largest using common numerators. *(Question 7)*
6. Students practice ordering fractions using various strategies. *(Question 8)*

Homework

1. Assign Homework *Questions 1–6* in the *Student Guide.*
2. Assign Part 3 of the Home Practice.

Assessment

Use Part 6 of the Home Practice as an assessment.

Answer Key is on pages 82–84.

Notes:

Study the following data table. Look for patterns within each column.

Fractions near or equal to 0	Fractions near or equal to $\frac{1}{2}$	Fractions near or equal to 1	Fractions much greater than 1
$\frac{0}{8}, \frac{2}{12}, \frac{1}{8}$	$\frac{3}{8}, \frac{4}{8}, \frac{2}{4}, \frac{7}{12}, \frac{4}{10}$	$\frac{5}{6}, \frac{8}{8}, \frac{9}{8}$	$\frac{16}{8}, \frac{19}{10}$

Use the table above or the Number Lines for Fractohoppers chart on the previous page to help you complete the following questions.

1. Make a table like the one above. Sort the following fractions in your table.
   $\frac{11}{12}, \frac{0}{12}, \frac{5}{12}, \frac{25}{12}, \frac{1}{12}, \frac{10}{12}$.

2. **A.** How are the fractions near 0 alike?
   B. How are the fractions near $\frac{1}{2}$ alike?
   C. How are the fractions near 1 alike?
   D. How can you tell if a fraction is greater than 1?

3. Add these fractions to your table: $\frac{2}{4}, \frac{1}{10}, \frac{24}{6}, \frac{1}{11}, \frac{6}{10}, \frac{5}{8}, \frac{2}{10}, \frac{7}{8}$, and $\frac{17}{10}$.

4. Add these fractions to your table: $\frac{14}{15}, \frac{11}{20}, \frac{1}{9}, \frac{103}{100}, \frac{40}{20}, \frac{23}{40}, \frac{3}{20}$, and $\frac{60}{100}$.

5. Write each of the following sets of fractions in order from smallest to largest. Use the symbol for "less than" (<) in your answer. Follow the example:
   Example: $\frac{2}{12}, \frac{19}{10}, \frac{4}{8}, \frac{5}{6}$ Answer: $\frac{2}{12} < \frac{4}{8} < \frac{5}{6} < \frac{19}{10}$
   A. $\frac{5}{12}, \frac{1}{10}, \frac{5}{6}, \frac{9}{8}$ **B.** $\frac{4}{5}, \frac{3}{6}, \frac{5}{4}, \frac{0}{2}$
   C. $\frac{12}{10}, \frac{10}{12}, \frac{7}{12}, \frac{1}{6}$ **D.** $\frac{20}{10}, \frac{1}{20}, \frac{7}{8}, \frac{3}{5}$

6. Write each of the following sets of fractions in order from smallest to largest. Use the symbol for "less than" (<) in your answer. Follow the example:
   Example: $\frac{2}{8}, \frac{7}{8}, \frac{5}{8}, \frac{1}{8}$ Answer: $\frac{1}{8} < \frac{2}{8} < \frac{5}{8} < \frac{7}{8}$
   A. $\frac{4}{5}, \frac{1}{5}, \frac{6}{5}, \frac{3}{5}$ **B.** $\frac{11}{12}, \frac{2}{12}, \frac{8}{12}, \frac{7}{12}$
   C. If two or more fractions have the same denominator, how can you tell which of the fractions is larger?

Comparing Fractions   SG • Grade 5 • Unit 3 • Lesson 4   **83**

Student Guide - page 83

1.

Fractions near or equal to 0	Fractions near or equal to $\frac{1}{2}$	Fractions near or equal to 1	Fractions much greater than 1
$\frac{0}{12}, \frac{1}{12}$	$\frac{5}{12}$	$\frac{10}{12}, \frac{11}{12}$	$\frac{25}{12}$

2.* **A.** The numerators are much smaller than the denominators.

   B. The numerators are about one-half the denominators.

   C. The numerators are almost the same as the denominators.

   D. The numerator is greater than the denominator.

3.

Fractions near or equal to 0	Fractions near or equal to $\frac{1}{2}$	Fractions near or equal to 1	Fractions much greater than 1
$\frac{0}{12}, \frac{1}{12}, \frac{1}{10}, \frac{1}{11}, \frac{2}{10}$	$\frac{5}{12}, \frac{2}{4}, \frac{6}{10}, \frac{5}{8}$	$\frac{10}{12}, \frac{11}{12}, \frac{7}{8}$	$\frac{25}{12}, \frac{24}{6}, \frac{17}{10}$

4.

Fractions near or equal to 0	Fractions near or equal to $\frac{1}{2}$	Fractions near or equal to 1	Fractions much greater than 1
$\frac{0}{12}, \frac{1}{12}, \frac{1}{10}, \frac{1}{11},$ $\frac{2}{10}, \frac{1}{9}, \frac{3}{20}$	$\frac{5}{12}, \frac{2}{4}, \frac{6}{10}, \frac{5}{8},$ $\frac{11}{20}, \frac{20}{40}, \frac{60}{100}$	$\frac{10}{12}, \frac{11}{12}, \frac{7}{8},$ $\frac{14}{15}, \frac{103}{100}$	$\frac{25}{12}, \frac{24}{6}, \frac{17}{10}, \frac{40}{20}$

5. **A.** $\frac{1}{10} < \frac{5}{12} < \frac{5}{6} < \frac{9}{8}$

   B. $\frac{0}{2} < \frac{3}{6} < \frac{4}{5} < \frac{5}{4}$

   C. $\frac{1}{6} < \frac{7}{12} < \frac{10}{12} < \frac{12}{10}$

   D. $\frac{1}{20} < \frac{3}{5} < \frac{7}{8} < \frac{20}{10}$

6. **A.** $\frac{1}{5} < \frac{3}{5} < \frac{4}{5} < \frac{6}{5}$

   B. $\frac{2}{12} < \frac{7}{12} < \frac{8}{12} < \frac{11}{12}$

   C. The fraction with the larger numerator is the larger fraction.*

*Answers and/or discussion are included in the Lesson Guide.

Student Guide (p. 84)

7. A. $\frac{1}{10} < \frac{1}{4} < \frac{1}{3} < \frac{1}{2}$ **B.** $\frac{3}{10} < \frac{3}{8} < \frac{3}{5} < \frac{3}{2}$

   C. The fraction with the smaller denominator is the larger fraction.*

8. A. $\frac{1}{12} < \frac{3}{8} < \frac{7}{12} < \frac{10}{10}$ **B.** $\frac{2}{9} < \frac{4}{8} < \frac{8}{14} < \frac{12}{11}$

   C. $\frac{7}{11} < \frac{7}{9} < \frac{7}{8} < \frac{7}{4}$ **D.** $\frac{1}{6} < \frac{3}{6} < \frac{5}{6} < \frac{9}{6}$

   E. $\frac{2}{12} < \frac{2}{4} < \frac{4}{6} < \frac{20}{10}$ **F.** $\frac{1}{10} < \frac{4}{9} < \frac{7}{10} < \frac{10}{9}$

Homework

Solution strategies will vary for *Questions 1–6.*

1. $\frac{2}{12} < \frac{2}{10} < \frac{2}{5} < \frac{2}{3}$

2. $\frac{1}{12} < \frac{3}{6} < \frac{7}{8} < \frac{13}{5}$

3. $\frac{2}{10} < \frac{3}{10} < \frac{5}{10} < \frac{7}{10}$

4. $\frac{0}{3} < \frac{1}{3} < \frac{4}{9} < \frac{11}{12}$

5. $\frac{5}{12} < \frac{5}{9} < \frac{5}{6} < \frac{5}{4}$

6. A. Brandon has the shortest walk.

   B. David has the longest walk.

Student Guide - page 84

Discovery Assignment Book (p. 28)

Home Practice†

Part 3. Fractions

1. Answers will vary. One possible solution is $\frac{2}{6}$.

2. Answers will vary. One possible solution is $\frac{2}{3}$.

3. Answers will vary. One possible solution is $\frac{1}{4}$.

4. Answers will vary. One possible solution is $\frac{5}{8}$.

5. Answers will vary. One possible solution is $\frac{7}{8}$.

6. A. $\frac{1}{10}$

   B. $\frac{5}{8}$

   C. $\frac{7}{6}$

   D. $\frac{8}{10}$

Discovery Assignment Book - page 28

*Answers and/or discussion are included in the Lesson Guide.
†Answers for all the Home Practice in the *Discovery Assignment Book* are at the end of the unit.

Discovery Assignment Book (p. 30)

Name _____ Date _____

1. Complete the following number sentences. The Number Lines for Fractohoppers chart you completed in Lesson 3 or the chart in Lesson 4 of the *Student Guide* may help you solve some of the problems.

   A. $\frac{1}{3} = \frac{2}{n}$ B. $\frac{9}{12} = \frac{n}{4}$ C. $\frac{2}{6} = \frac{n}{12}$

   D. $\frac{5}{8} = \frac{15}{n}$ E. $\frac{20}{70} = \frac{n}{7}$ F. $\frac{7}{9} = \frac{n}{36}$

   G. $\frac{3}{5} = \frac{n}{25}$ H. $\frac{4}{40} = \frac{1}{n}$ I. $\frac{2}{3} = \frac{8}{n}$

2. Write each mixed number as an improper fraction.

   A. $1\frac{1}{4}$ B. $5\frac{2}{3}$ C. $2\frac{7}{8}$ D. $3\frac{3}{5}$

3. Write each improper fraction as a mixed number.

   A. $\frac{9}{4}$ B. $\frac{20}{6}$ C. $\frac{21}{2}$ D. $\frac{23}{12}$

4. Put each of the following sets of fractions in order from smallest to largest.

   A. $\frac{9}{5}, \frac{9}{10}, \frac{9}{2}, \frac{9}{12}$ B. $\frac{5}{6}, \frac{8}{7}, \frac{7}{12}, \frac{1}{8}$

   C. $\frac{6}{6}, \frac{3}{6}, \frac{10}{6}, \frac{2}{6}$ D. $\frac{3}{20}, \frac{3}{2}, \frac{9}{11}, \frac{9}{16}$

30 DAB • Grade 5 • Unit 3   FRACTIONS AND RATIOS

Discovery Assignment Book - page 30

Discovery Assignment Book (p. 30)

Part 6. A Fraction More

1. A. $\frac{1}{3} = \frac{2}{6}$

   B. $\frac{9}{12} = \frac{3}{4}$

   C. $\frac{2}{6} = \frac{4}{12}$

   D. $\frac{5}{8} = \frac{15}{24}$

   E. $\frac{20}{70} = \frac{2}{7}$

   F. $\frac{7}{9} = \frac{28}{36}$

   G. $\frac{3}{5} = \frac{15}{25}$

   H. $\frac{4}{40} = \frac{1}{10}$

   I. $\frac{2}{3} = \frac{8}{12}$

2. A. $\frac{5}{4}$

   B. $\frac{17}{3}$

   C. $\frac{23}{8}$

   D. $\frac{18}{5}$

3. A. $2\frac{1}{4}$

   B. $3\frac{2}{6}$ or $3\frac{1}{3}$

   C. $10\frac{1}{2}$

   D. $1\frac{11}{12}$

4. A. $\frac{9}{12}, \frac{9}{10}, \frac{9}{5}, \frac{9}{2}$

   B. $\frac{1}{8}, \frac{7}{12}, \frac{5}{6}, \frac{8}{7}$

   C. $\frac{2}{6}, \frac{3}{6}, \frac{6}{6}, \frac{10}{6}$

   D. $\frac{3}{20}, \frac{9}{16}, \frac{9}{11}, \frac{3}{2}$

Using Ratios

Lesson Overview

Estimated Class Sessions
2-3

Students learn to use ratios in the context of a school Fun Fair. They use ratios to produce patterns that help them find the cost of multiple items at a bake sale. They express ratios in words, tables, graphs, and fractions.

Key Content

- Using words, tables, graphs, and fractions to express ratios.
- Finding equal ratios.
- Using ratios to solve problems.

Key Vocabulary

- ratio

Math Facts

Review the multiplication and division facts for the 2s and 3s. Complete DPP item K.

Homework

1. Assign the homework at the end of the lesson. Students will need enough graph paper to make three or four graphs.
2. Assign Part 5 of the Home Practice.

Assessment

1. Use **Question 1** in the Homework section of the *Student Guide*.
2. Use the *Quiz Time* Assessment Pages.

Curriculum Sequence

Before This Unit

In third and fourth grade, students used point graphs to solve problems. For specific examples in fourth grade, see the labs *Perimeter vs. Length* (Unit 2), *Bouncing Ball* (Unit 5), *Volume vs. Number* (Unit 8), *Downhill Racer* (Unit 10), and *Perimeter vs. Area* (Unit 16).

After This Unit

Students will have many opportunities to develop the concepts and skills presented in this lesson. In Unit 4, they use graphs and ratios to investigate the absorbency of paper towels in the lab *Spreading Out,* and in Unit 5, they use the same tools to compare speeds in the lab *A Day at the Races.* In Unit 13, students solve many problems involving ratios and proportions in various contexts.

Materials List

Supplies and Copies

Student	Teacher
Supplies for Each Student • ruler	**Supplies**
Copies • 1 copy of *Quiz Time* per student (*Unit Resource Guide* Pages 94–96) • 5 copies of *Centimeter Graph Paper* per student (*Unit Resource Guide* Page 100) • 1 copy of *Half-Centimeter Grid Paper* per student, optional (*Unit Resource Guide* Page 101)	**Copies/Transparencies** • 1 transparency of *Cost of Muffins Data Table* (*Unit Resource Guide* Page 97) • 1 transparency of *Cost of Muffins Graph* (*Unit Resource Guide* Page 98) • 1 transparency of *Using Ratios to Convert Feet to Yards* (*Unit Resource Guide* Page 99)

All blackline masters including assessment, transparency, and DPP masters are also on the Teacher Resource CD.

Student Books

Using Ratios (Student Guide Pages 85–93)

Daily Practice and Problems and Home Practice

DPP items K–N (*Unit Resource Guide* Pages 21–23)
Home Practice Part 5 (*Discovery Assignment Book* Page 29)

Note: Classrooms whose pacing differs significantly from the suggested pacing of the units should use the Math Facts Calendar in Section 4 of the *Facts Resource Guide* to ensure students receive the complete math facts program.

Daily Practice and Problems

Suggestions for using the DPPs are on page 91.

K. Bit: Fact Families for × and ÷
(URG p. 21)

Complete the number sentences for the related facts.

A. $5 \times 2 =$ ___   B. $8 \times 3 =$ ___

___ $\div 5 =$ ___   ___ $\div$ ___ $= 8$

___ $\div 2 =$ ___   ___ $\div 8 =$ ___

$2 \times$ ___ $=$ ___   ___ $\times 8 =$ ___

C. $18 \div 2 =$ ___   D. $3 \times$ ___ $= 6$

___ $\times 2 =$ ___ $6 \div$ ___ $=$ ___

$18 \div$ ___ $=$ ___ $6 \div$ ___ $=$ ___

$2 \times$ ___ $=$ ___   ___ $\times 3 =$ ___

L. Task: Multiplication Practice
(URG p. 22)

Solve the following problems using paper and pencil. Estimate to be sure your answers are reasonable.

A. $65 \times 27 =$ B. $58 \times 86 =$
C. $94 \times 8 =$ D. $69 \times 45 =$
E. $80 \times 46 =$ F. $937 \times 3 =$

M. Bit: Fractions to Order (URG p. 22)

Arrange the fractions below in order from smallest to largest. You may use the Number Lines for Fractohoppers chart in the *Student Guide* for Lesson 4.

$\frac{5}{6}$ $\frac{1}{4}$ $\frac{1}{6}$ $\frac{2}{5}$ $\frac{1}{3}$ $\frac{3}{4}$

N. Task: Pieces and Parts (URG p. 23)

Brandon says that $\frac{2}{5}$ is more than $\frac{1}{2}$ because $\frac{2}{5}$ has more pieces.

1. Is Brandon right or wrong?
2. Write a letter to Brandon explaining which is greater, $\frac{2}{5}$ or $\frac{1}{2}$, and why. Try to use a picture in your letter.

Lee Yah says that $\frac{1}{8}$ is more than $\frac{1}{6}$ because eight is more than six.

3. Is Lee Yah right or wrong?
4. Write a letter to Lee Yah explaining which is larger, $\frac{1}{6}$ or $\frac{1}{8}$, and why. Try to use a picture in your letter.

Using Ratios

The Fun Fair
Each year, the fifth-grade students at Bessie Coleman School organize a Fun Fair for the school. They plan games and sell refreshments. This year, Frank and Edward are in charge of the bake sale. Here is their price list:

Edward made the following table to help them find the cost of the muffins:

Edward's Table

Number of Muffins	Cost
1	30¢
2	60¢
3	90¢
4	$1.20

Edward said, "If we make a table like this one for everything we sell, we will be able to find the prices of things quickly. We can multiply or use patterns to fill in the tables."

Using Ratios   SG • Grade 5 • Unit 3 • Lesson 5   **85**

Student Guide - page 85

Frank thought for a few minutes and then he got a piece of graph paper and began to draw a graph. "You're right, a table will work, but we will have to figure out the whole table. Look at this graph. The points for one, two, and three muffins are in a line."

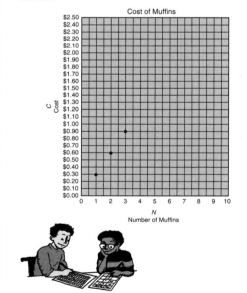

86   SG • Grade 5 • Unit 3 • Lesson 5   Using Ratios

Student Guide - page 86

Teaching the Activity

Part 1 **The Fun Fair: Using Tables and Graphs to Study Ratios**

The *Using Ratios* Activity Pages in the *Student Guide* describe how two students use tables and graphs to find the cost of multiple items at a bake sale. Specifically, one student builds a table to show the cost of one, two, three, and four muffins, and another student draws a graph with the same information. Begin the discussion using *Questions 1–2,* which ask students to describe patterns in the table. Students may observe that the numbers in the second column are multiples of 30¢ (often expressed as "counting by 30"); the cost of the muffins is 30 cents times the number of muffins; and doubling the number of muffins doubles the cost. Show students how to find this relationship on the graph.

> ### TIMS Tip
>
> The skills needed to answer **Questions 1–7** were introduced in third grade and applied in several labs and activities in fourth grade. These skills include plotting points, drawing a line to fit the points, and using the line to solve problems. If students used *Math Trailblazers* before, use these questions as review. If students are new to the curriculum, take more time teaching this lesson. Go through each of the steps involved in creating a point graph. Include labeling the axes, titling the graph, scaling correctly, and drawing a best-fit line.

Question 3 asks students to compare the patterns in the table to those in the graph. Use the *Cost of Muffins Data Table* and *Cost of Muffins Graph* Transparency Masters to discuss the table and review how to plot points for table entries. See Figure 10. Remind students that points are plotted by finding the number of muffins on the horizontal axis and the cost of the muffins on the vertical axis. The points fall on a line that reflects the pattern in the table. The table shows that as the number of muffins increases by one, the cost of the muffins increases by 30¢. Each point added to the graph moves the line to the right one (indicating an increase in the number of muffins by one) and moves the line up three spaces (indicating an increase in the cost of the muffins by 30¢, since each space stands for 10¢).

> ### Content Note
>
> **Cents.** As students answer questions that involve writing cents, make sure they write the cents appropriately. Thirty cents can be written as 30¢ or $0.30, not 0.30¢.

88   URG • Grade 5 • Unit 3 • Lesson 5

Cost of Muffins

Number of Muffins	Cost
1	30¢
2	60¢
3	90¢
4	$1.20

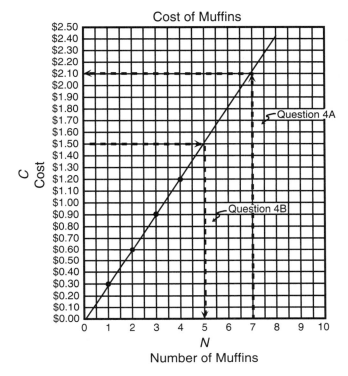

Figure 10: *Fitting a line to the points and using the line to answer questions*

Fit a line to the points as shown in Figure 10, emphasizing the importance of using a ruler to draw a straight line. Figure 10 also shows how to use the line to find the cost of seven muffins and find the number of muffins a customer can buy for $1.50 *(Question 4)*.

Questions 5–7 ask students to repeat the same process for a different ratio (2 cookies for 25¢). Students build a table, plot points, look for patterns, fit a line, and use the graph to answer questions. As students work through these problems, encourage them to describe their solution strategies and any patterns they observe. *Question 7B* illustrates the limitations of using the line to find prices. Drawing a line implies that all the points on the line, including those that correspond to fractions of a cent or fractions of a cookie, make sense. However, the point

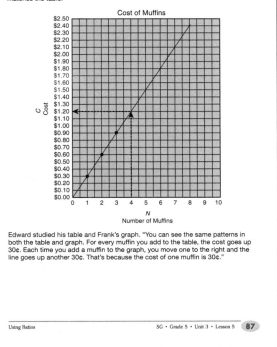

"If we use a ruler to draw the line, we can use the line to find the cost of different numbers of muffins. See, the line shows that 4 muffins will cost $1.20. That matches the table."

Edward studied his table and Frank's graph. "You can see the same patterns in both the table and graph. For every muffin you add to the table, the cost goes up 30¢. Each time you add a muffin to the graph, you move one to the right and the line goes up another 30¢. That's because the cost of one muffin is 30¢."

Student Guide - page 87

 **Discuss**

1. What patterns do you see in Edward's table?
2. How could you complete the table by using multiplication?
3. What patterns do you think Edward sees in both the table and graph? Describe the patterns in your own words.
4. **A.** Use the graph to find the cost of seven muffins.
   B. If a customer has $1.50, how many muffins can he or she buy?
5. **A.** Copy and complete the table for the cost of cookies.

Number of Cookies	Cost
2	25¢
6	
	$1.00

   B. Make a graph of the data. Graph the number of cookies on the horizontal axis and the cost on the vertical axis.
6. **A.** What patterns do you see in the table in Question 5?
   B. What patterns do you see in the graph?
   C. Describe any patterns you see in both the table and graph.
7. **A.** Use your graph in Question 5B to find the cost of 1 dozen (12) cookies.
   B. What is the cost of three cookies?

Student Guide - page 88 (Answers on p. 102)

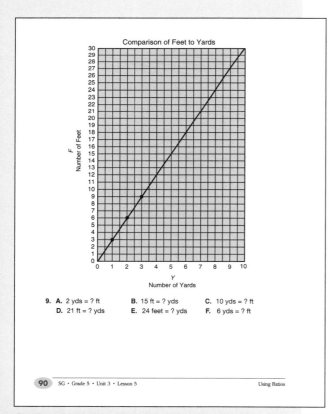

Ratios

Edward and Frank used ratios to help them with the prices for the bake sale. A **ratio** is a way to compare two numbers or quantities. When they were finding out prices of muffins they used the ratio "1 muffin costs 30 cents." They found equal ratios: "2 muffins cost 60 cents" and "3 muffins cost 90 cents."

8. Use your table or graph in Question 5 to name two ratios equal to the ratio "2 cookies for 25¢."

The decorating committee plans to decorate the gym with crepe paper, ribbon, and balloons.

The committee measured the length and width of the gym in yards. They measured the height of the booths in feet. When they went to the store, they found that ribbon is sold by the yard. Crepe paper is sold by the foot. One way to convert feet to yards and yards to feet is by using a graph. The students made a graph that compares feet to yards and yards to feet. It is on the following page.

Using Ratios   SG • Grade 5 • Unit 3 • Lesson 5   **89**

Student Guide - page 89 *(Answers on p. 103)*

Comparison of Feet to Yards

9. A. 2 yds = ? ft   **B.** 15 ft = ? yds   **C.** 10 yds = ? ft
   D. 21 ft = ? yds   **E.** 24 feet = ? yds   **F.** 6 yds = ? ft

90   SG • Grade 5 • Unit 3 • Lesson 5   Using Ratios

Student Guide - page 90 *(Answers on p. 103)*

on the line corresponding to three cookies shows a cost of $37\frac{1}{2}$ cents. Since it is not possible to collect a half penny, charging $37\frac{1}{2}$ cents is not realistic, so the students at the bake sale would probably charge 38 cents.

Part 2 Ratios

In the Ratios section in the *Student Guide,* students use words and symbols to express ratios and to show equivalence between ratios. In **Question 8** they use words to name ratios equal to "2 cookies for 25¢" and in **Questions 9–11** they use a graph to find ratios equal to $\frac{3 \text{ feet}}{1 \text{ yard}}$ and write them as fractions. The *Using Ratios to Convert Feet to Yards* Transparency allows you to show students how to use the graph to convert feet to yards and yards to feet and how to write equal ratios using points on the line.

It is important that students make connections between the various representations of ratios (words, tables, graphs, and symbols), so they can use them as tools to solve problems. Equal ratios can be shown as entries in a table, points on a straight line that goes through (0,0), and equivalent fractions. **Question 12** is designed to help students see these connections. They must decide if $\frac{25¢}{2 \text{ cookies}}$ is equal to $\frac{15¢}{1 \text{ cookie}}$ (**Question 12A**). It should be clear to students

Ratios. According to Webster's Dictionary, a **ratio** is "the indicated quotient of two mathematical expressions." For example, "twenty miles per gallon" is a ratio, namely "twenty miles to one gallon." We often write ratios as fractions, such as $\frac{20 \text{ miles}}{1 \text{ gallon}}$. When the dictionary says "indicated quotient," it means that the division is not actually performed (unless needed). For example, you might find that the ratio of miles to gallons for your car is $\frac{160 \text{ miles}}{8 \text{ gallons}}$. When you carry out the division of 160 by 8 you see that this ratio is the same as $\frac{20 \text{ miles}}{1 \text{ gallon}}$. This is one example of a general rule for telling when two ratios are equal.

Two ratios are equal if the fractions are equivalent. Alternatively, two ratios are equal if the result of the divisions are the same. For example, $\frac{\$3}{4 \text{ pumpkins}} = \frac{\$9}{12 \text{ pumpkins}}$ because the fractions $\frac{3}{4}$ and $\frac{9}{12}$ are equal. Alternatively, dividing 3 by 4 and dividing 9 by 12 both give 0.75.

that the fractions are not equivalent ($\frac{25¢}{2 \text{ cookies}} \neq \frac{15¢}{1 \text{ cookie}}$) since doubling the number of cookies does not double the cost. **Question 12B** asks students to add a point for the ratio $\frac{15¢}{1 \text{ cookie}}$ to the graph they made in **Question 5.** This point does not lie on the line since the line is made up of points with ratios equivalent to $\frac{25¢}{2 \text{ cookies}}$. This is an example of the general principle that points will lie on the same line through (0,0) only when the ratios are equal.

Content Note

Proportions. A proportion is a statement of equality between two ratios. Although the term *proportion* will be introduced in a later unit, students use proportional reasoning throughout this lesson. Proportional reasoning is an important theme across the *Math Trailblazers* curriculum, especially in the third, fourth, and fifth grades. Students encounter proportions in many representations: concrete materials, real-life situations, tables, graphs, and symbols. They make connections between these representations and use them as tools to solve problems that require proportional thinking.

Math Facts

Use DPP item K to write fact families for the 2s and 3s.

Homework and Practice

- Assign the homework at the end of the lesson. Students will need enough graph paper to make three or four graphs.

- Assign DPP items L, M, and N for work with multiplication and fractions.

- Assign Part 5 of the Home Practice in the *Discovery Assignment Book* for homework. Students will need a piece of graph paper and a ruler to complete this section.

Answers for Part 5 of the Home Practice are in the Answer Key at the end of this lesson and at the end of this unit.

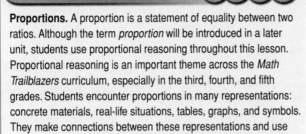

Ratios can be written as fractions. To compare feet and yards, we can write the ratio $\frac{3 \text{ ft}}{1 \text{ yd}}$. We can write number sentences using fractions that show ratios are equal. When the fractions are equal, the ratios are equal:

$$\frac{3 \text{ ft}}{1 \text{ yd}} = \frac{6 \text{ ft}}{2 \text{ yds}} \text{ and } \frac{3 \text{ ft}}{1 \text{ yd}} = \frac{15 \text{ ft}}{5 \text{ yds}}$$

10. Complete the following number sentence: $\frac{3 \text{ ft}}{1 \text{ yd}} = \frac{21 \text{ ft}}{? \text{ yds}}$.

You can also compare feet to yards by looking at the ratio of yards to feet. For example:

$$\frac{1 \text{ yd}}{3 \text{ ft}} = \frac{2 \text{ yds}}{6 \text{ ft}} = \frac{5 \text{ yds}}{15 \text{ ft}}$$

11. Using fractions, write two other ratios that are equal to $\frac{3 \text{ ft}}{1 \text{ yd}}$.

12. Edward and Frank decided to sell 1 cookie for 15¢.
    A. Are the following two ratios equal? Why or why not?

    $$\frac{25¢}{2 \text{ cookies}} \text{ and } \frac{15¢}{1 \text{ cookie}}$$

    B. Add a point to the graph you made for Question 5 which shows that 1 cookie costs 15¢. Is this point on your line? Why or why not?

13. Using fractions, write two ratios that are equal to $\frac{30¢}{1 \text{ muffin}}$.

14. Using fractions, write two ratios equal to $\frac{25¢}{2 \text{ cookies}}$.

Using Ratios   SG • Grade 5 • Unit 3 • Lesson 5   **91**

Student Guide - page 91 *(Answers on p. 104)*

Name _____ Date _____

PART 5 **Exercising at the Gym**
You will need a piece of graph paper to complete this part.

Irma's mother exercises on a stair-step machine for 18 minutes. She exercises at the same rate for the entire time. The following data table shows how many calories she burned at various times.

Time T	Calories Burned C
1	9
5	45
10	90
12	108
18	162

1. Make a point graph of the data on a piece of graph paper. Graph time on the horizontal axis. Be sure to label the axes and to give your graph a title.

2. Use a ruler to fit a line to the points.

3. About how many calories did Irma's mother burn after 15 minutes? How did you decide?

4. About how long did it take her to burn 100 calories? How did you decide?

5. A. Choose a point on the graph and use it to write a ratio of calories burned to time taken. (Be sure to include units.)

   B. Write two more ratios equal to the ratio in Question 5A.

   C. If Irma's mother exercised at the same rate for 30 minutes on the stair-step machine, how many calories would she burn? Explain your solution.

FRACTIONS AND RATIOS   DAB • Grade 5 • Unit 3   **29**

Discovery Assignment Book - page 29 *(Answers on p. 107)*

Student Guide - page 92 *(Answers on pp. 104–105)*

Student Guide - page 93 *(Answers on p. 106)*

- Use **Question 1** in the Homework section to see if students can build tables, draw graphs, and use fractions to represent equal ratios.
- Use the *Quiz Time* Assessment Pages to quiz students on concepts in the first five lessons of this unit.

Extension

Have students look at newspaper or magazine articles, find ratios, and write equivalent fractions for the ratios they find. Students can also look for ratios in stores,

Literature Connection

- Xiong, Blip. *Nine in One, Grr! Grr!* Children's Book Press, San Francisco, 1989.

  This book is a retelling of a folktale of the Hmong people of Laos. It tells the story of a tiger who is promised nine cubs each year by the great god Shao. The other animals are worried that there will be too many tigers on the earth, so they change the promise to one cub every nine years. Thus, the book can be used to illustrate the difference between the ratios of 9 to 1 and 1 to 9. After reading the story, ask the class how many offspring the mother tiger would have after 9 years if the ratio were $\frac{9 \text{ cubs}}{1 \text{ year}}$ and how many cubs she would have after 9 years with a ratio of $\frac{1 \text{ cub}}{9 \text{ years}}$.

Journal Prompt

Which of the following is the easiest way for you to find equal ratios: building tables, drawing graphs, or finding equivalent fractions? Why do you think so?

At a Glance

Math Facts and Daily Practice and Problems

1. Review the multiplication and division facts for the 2s and 3s.
2. Complete DPP items K–N.

Part 1. The Fun Fair: Using Tables and Graphs to Study Ratios

1. Students read The Fun Fair section on the *Using Ratios Activity* Pages in the *Student Guide* and study the table and graph that show the prices for different numbers of muffins. *(Questions 1–2)*
2. Students look for patterns in the table.
3. Use the *Cost of Muffins Graph* Transparency Master to review plotting points and fitting a line to the points.
4. Students compare the patterns in the table to the patterns in the graph and discuss *Questions 3–7*.
5. Students complete a data table and graph that show the prices for different numbers of cookies. *(Question 5)*. They discuss patterns in *Question 6* and use the data table and graph to answer *Question 7*.

Part 2. Ratios

1. Students read and discuss the text and questions in the Ratios section in the *Student Guide*. *(Questions 8–11)*
2. Use the *Using Ratios to Convert Feet to Yards* Transparency Master to show students how to use the graph to convert feet to yards and yards to feet and how to write equal ratios using points on a straight line through (0,0).
3. Students complete *Questions 12–14* in the *Student Guide* that explore new ratios and lines on graphs.

Homework

1. Assign the homework at the end of the lesson. Students will need enough graph paper to make three or four graphs.
2. Assign Part 5 of the Home Practice.

Assessment

1. Use *Question 1* in the Homework section of the *Student Guide*.
2. Use the *Quiz Time* Assessment Pages.

Extension

Have students find ratios and write equivalent fractions.

Connection

Read and discuss *Nine in One, Grr! Grr!* by Blip Xiong.

Answer Key is on pages 102–109.

Notes:

Quiz Time

You will need pattern blocks to complete this quiz.

1. **A.** If the blue rhombus is $\frac{1}{2}$, sketch and label one whole.

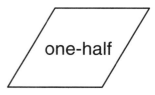

   B. Which block shows $\frac{1}{4}$?

   C. Write a number for 3 purple triangles.

   D. Write a number for one yellow hexagon.

2. Show $\frac{2}{3}$ using blue and at least one other color pattern block. The yellow hexagon is one whole. Sketch your figure and write a number sentence for it.

Assessment Blackline Master

3. A. Write $\frac{17}{3}$ as a mixed number.

B. Write $2\frac{5}{6}$ as an improper fraction.

4. Put each of the following sets of fractions in order from smallest to largest.

A. $\frac{7}{8}, \frac{1}{8}, \frac{9}{8}$

B. $\frac{3}{5}, \frac{1}{10}, \frac{4}{9}, \frac{3}{2}$

C. $\frac{1}{2}, \frac{1}{8}, \frac{1}{4}$

5. Complete the following number sentences:

A. $\frac{5}{3} = \frac{?}{12}$

B. $\frac{3}{4} = \frac{15}{?}$

6. Frank wrote the following number sentence: $\frac{20¢}{3 \text{ cookies}} = \frac{10¢}{2 \text{ cookies}}$.
Is the number sentence true? Why or why not?

7. Ming showed the cost of cookies on a graph.

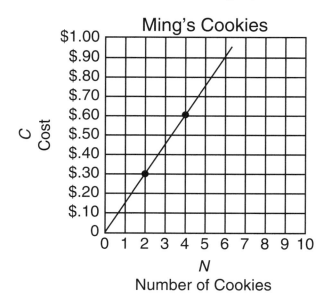

A. How much do 3 cookies cost?

B. How much does 1 cookie cost?

C. Write a ratio of cost for 6 cookies.

D. How many of Ming's cookies can you buy with $3.00?

E. Maya bought 9 cookies for 90 cents. Does this ratio belong on Ming's graph? Explain.

Cost of Muffins Data Table

Number of Muffins	Cost
1	30¢
2	60¢
3	90¢
4	$1.20

Cost of Muffins Graph

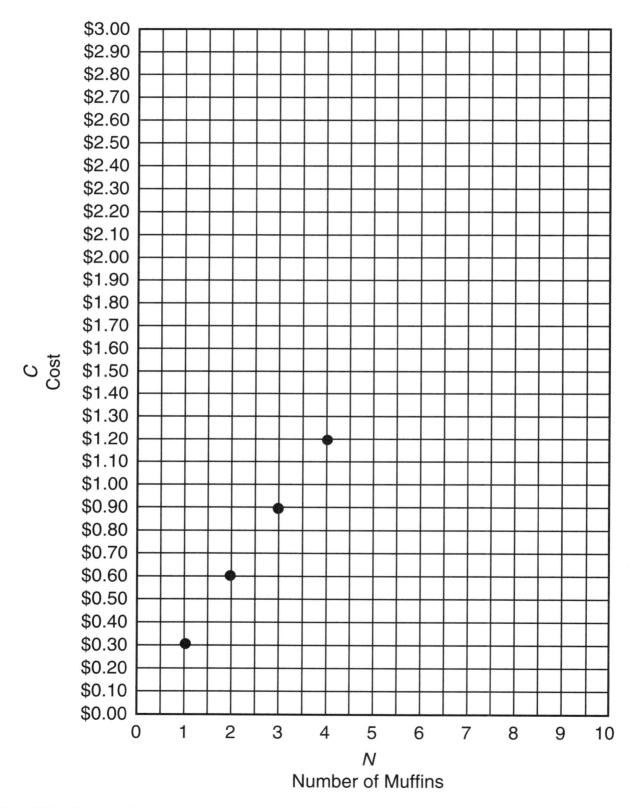

C
Cost

N
Number of Muffins

Transparency Master

Using Ratios to
Convert Feet to Yards

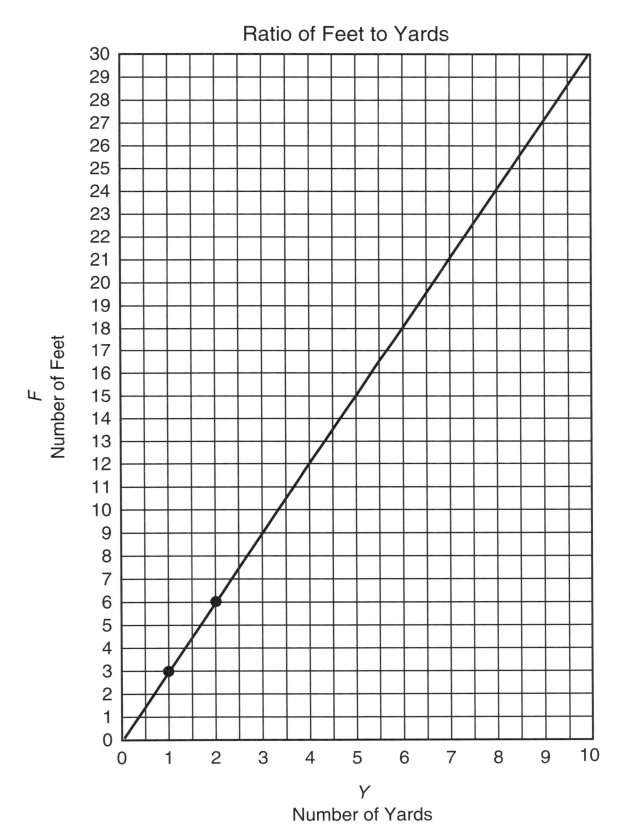

Ratio of Feet to Yards

F
Number of Feet

Y
Number of Yards

Name _____   Date _____

Centimeter Graph Paper, Blackline Master

Name _____ Date _____

Half-Centimeter Grid Paper

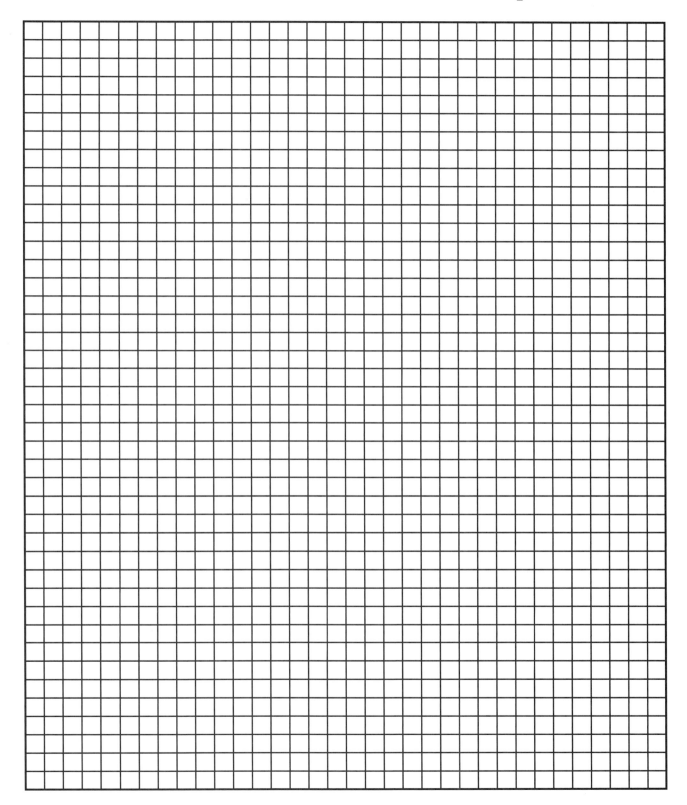

1. What patterns do you see in Edward's table?

2. How could you complete the table by using multiplication?

3. What patterns do you think Edward sees in both the table and graph? Describe the patterns in your own words.

4. **A.** Use the graph to find the cost of seven muffins.
   B. If a customer has $1.50, how many muffins can he or she buy?

5. **A.** Copy and complete the table for the cost of cookies.

Number of Cookies	Cost
2	25¢
6	
	$1.00

   B. Make a graph of the data. Graph the number of cookies on the horizontal axis and the cost on the vertical axis.

6. **A.** What patterns do you see in the table in Question 5?
   B. What patterns do you see in the graph?
   C. Describe any patterns you see in both the table and graph.

7. **A.** Use your graph in Question 5B to find the cost of 1 dozen (12) cookies.
   B. What is the cost of three cookies?

Student Guide - page 88

Student Guide (p. 88)

1. Answers will vary. Some possible patterns include: the numbers in the second column are multiples of 30¢, the cost of the muffins is 30¢ times the number of muffins, doubling the number of muffins doubles the cost, etc.*

2. Answers will vary. Students can double the number of muffins, which doubles the cost or they can multiply the number of muffins by 30¢.*

3. Answers will vary. The table and graph show that as the number of muffins increases by one, the cost of the muffins increases by 30¢.*

4.* **A.** $2.10; See the graph in Figure 10 in Lesson Guide 5.
   B. 5 muffins; See the graph in Figure 10 in Lesson Guide 5.

5. **A.**

Number of Cookies	Cost
2	25¢
4	50¢
6	75¢
8	$1.00

   B.

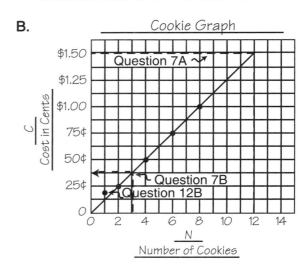

Cookie Graph

6. **A.** Answers will vary. Some possible patterns include: the numbers in the second column are multiples of 25¢, doubling the number of muffins doubles the cost, etc.

   B. Answers will vary. Students should see similar patterns in the graph as in the table. As the number of cookies increases by two, the cost increases by 25¢.

   C. Answers will vary. The table and graph show that as the number of cookies doubles, so does the cost. As the number of cookies increases by two, the cost increases by 25¢.

7. **A.** $1.50
   B. $37\frac{1}{2}$ cents or more practically, 38¢*

*Answers and/or discussion are included in the Lesson Guide.

Student Guide (p. 89)

8. Answers will vary. Two possible ratios include: 4 cookies for 50¢ and 6 cookies for 75¢.

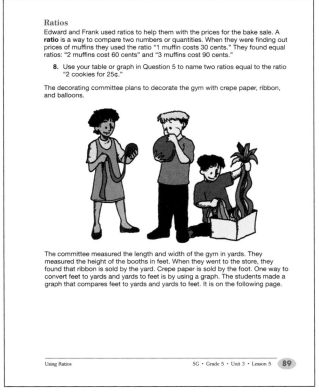

Student Guide - page 89

Student Guide (p. 90)

9. **A.** 6 feet

B. 5 yards

C. 30 feet

D. 7 yards

E. 8 yards

F. $7\frac{1}{3}$ yards*

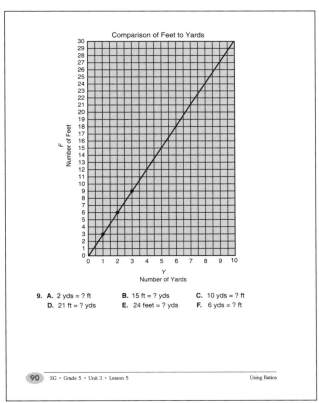

Student Guide - page 90

*Answers and/or discussion are included in the Lesson Guide.

Ratios can be written as fractions. To compare feet and yards, we can write the ratio $\frac{3\,ft}{1\,yd}$. We can write number sentences using fractions that show ratios are equal. When the fractions are equal, the ratios are equal:

$$\frac{3\,ft}{1\,yd} = \frac{6\,ft}{2\,yds} \text{ and } \frac{3\,ft}{1\,yd} = \frac{15\,ft}{5\,yds}$$

10. Complete the following number sentence: $\frac{3\,ft}{1\,yd} = \frac{21\,ft}{?\,yds}$.

You can also compare feet to yards by looking at the ratio of yards to feet. For example:

$$\frac{1\,yd}{3\,ft} = \frac{2\,yds}{6\,ft} = \frac{5\,yds}{15\,ft}$$

11. Using fractions, write two other ratios that are equal to $\frac{3\,ft}{1\,yd}$.

12. Edward and Frank decided to sell 1 cookie for 15¢.
    A. Are the following two ratios equal? Why or why not?

$$\frac{25¢}{2\text{ cookies}} \text{ and } \frac{15¢}{1\text{ cookie}}$$

    B. Add a point to the graph you made for Question 5 which shows that 1 cookie costs 15¢. Is this point on your line? Why or why not?

13. Using fractions, write two ratios that are equal to $\frac{30¢}{1\text{ muffin}}$.

14. Using fractions, write two ratios equal to $\frac{25¢}{2\text{ cookies}}$.

Using Ratios   SG • Grade 5 • Unit 3 • Lesson 5   **91**

Student Guide - page 91

You will need enough graph paper to make two graphs.

1. A. The fifth graders decided to make data tables to help the first graders use coins to pay for games and food at the fun fair. Copy and complete the tables on your paper. Fill in at least 5 rows in each table.

Number of Nickels	Number of Dimes
2	1

Number of Quarters	Number of Dimes
2	5
4	

   B. Make a graph that compares the value of dimes to the value of nickels. (Put the number of nickels on the horizontal axis and the number of dimes on the vertical axis.)

   C. Use fractions to write three ratios equal to $\frac{1\text{ dime}}{2\text{ nickels}}$.

   D. Make a graph that compares the value of dimes to the value of quarters. (Put quarters on the horizontal axis.)

   E. Use fractions to write three ratios equal to $\frac{5\text{ dimes}}{2\text{ quarters}}$.

2. There are four quarts in a gallon.
   A. Make a table with at least 5 rows that can be used to convert quarts to gallons.
   B. Write three ratios equal to $\frac{4\text{ quarts}}{1\text{ gallon}}$.

3. The poster for the bake sale says that one dozen rolls cost $2.40.
   A. How much will three dozen rolls cost?
   B. How much will six rolls cost? Explain how you found your answer.

92   SG • Grade 5 • Unit 3 • Lesson 5   Using Ratios

Student Guide - page 92

*Answers and/or discussion are included in the Lesson Guide.

Student Guide (p. 91)

10. 7 yards

11. Answers will vary. Two possible ratios include:
    $\frac{9\text{ feet}}{3\text{ yards}}$ and $\frac{18\text{ feet}}{6\text{ yards}}$.

12.* A. No, 1 cookie for 15¢ means 2 cookies for 30¢.

    B. No, the point falls on the line only if the ratio is equal.

13. Answers will vary. Two possible ratios include:
    $\frac{60¢}{2\text{ muffins}}$ and $\frac{90¢}{3\text{ muffins}}$.

14. Answers will vary. Two possible ratios include:
    $\frac{50¢}{4\text{ cookies}}$ and $\frac{75¢}{6\text{ cookies}}$.

Student Guide (p. 92)

Homework

1. A.

Number of Nickels	Number of Dimes
2	1
4	2
6	3
8	4
10	5

Number of Quarters	Number of Dimes
2	5
4	10
6	15
8	20
10	25

B.

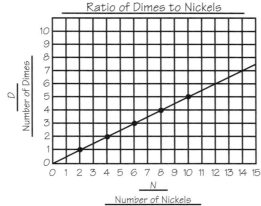

Ratio of Dimes to Nickels

C. Answers will vary. Three possible ratios
include: $\frac{2 \text{ dimes}}{4 \text{ nickels}}$, $\frac{3 \text{ dimes}}{6 \text{ nickels}}$, and $\frac{4 \text{ dimes}}{8 \text{ nickels}}$.

D.

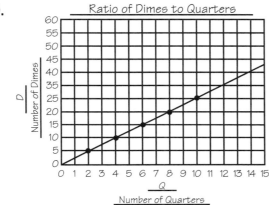

Ratio of Dimes to Quarters

E. Answers will vary. Three possible ratios
include: $\frac{10 \text{ dimes}}{4 \text{ quarters}}$, $\frac{15 \text{ dimes}}{6 \text{ quarters}}$, and $\frac{20 \text{ dimes}}{8 \text{ quarters}}$.

2. A.

Gallons	Quarts
1	4
2	8
3	12
4	16
5	20

B. Answers will vary. Three possible ratios
include: $\frac{8 \text{ quarts}}{2 \text{ gallons}}$, $\frac{12 \text{ quarts}}{3 \text{ gallons}}$, and $\frac{16 \text{ quarts}}{4 \text{ gallons}}$.

3. A. $7.20

B. $1.20; explanations will vary. One possible
explanation is to take half of $2.40 since
6 rolls is half of one dozen.

4. The poster for the bake sale says that brownies cost 50¢ each or 3 for $1.00.
   A. Write a fraction that shows the cost of one brownie as a ratio of cost to the number of brownies.
   B. Write a fraction that shows the cost of three brownies as a ratio of cost to the number of brownies.
   C. Are the ratios in Parts A and B equal? Why or why not?

Use the graph below to answer the following questions.

5. A. What is the cost for three people to see a movie?
   B. What is the cost for six people to see a movie?
   C. A customer paid the ticket seller $35.00. How many tickets did he or she buy?
   D. Choose a point on the graph, and write a ratio that shows the cost to the number of people.
   E. Write two other ratios equal to the ratio you wrote in Part D.

Movie Prices

Graph: y-axis labeled C / Cost, values from $5.00 to $50.00; x-axis labeled N / Number of People, values 0 to 12.

Student Guide - page 93

Student Guide (p. 93)

4. A. $\frac{\$0.50}{1 \text{ brownie}}$ or $\frac{50¢}{1 \text{ brownie}}$

   B. $\frac{\$1.00}{3 \text{ brownies}}$

   C. No, 3 brownies should cost $1.50 according to the ratio $\frac{\$0.50}{1 \text{ brownie}}$, but 3 brownies actually cost $1.00.

5. A. $15.00

   B. $30.00

   C. 7 tickets

   D. Answers will vary. One possible ratio is $\frac{\$5.00}{1 \text{ person}}$.

   E. Answers will vary. Two possible ratios include: $\frac{\$10.00}{2 \text{ people}}$ and $\frac{\$15.00}{3 \text{ people}}$.

Discovery Assignment Book (p. 29)

Home Practice*

Part 5. Exercising at the Gym

1.–2.

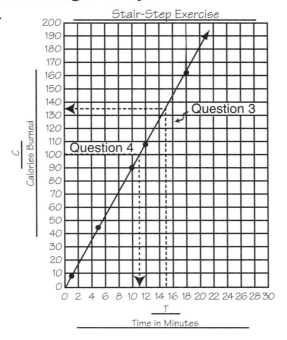

3. About 135 calories. Answers will vary slightly. Students can show their work on the graph.

4. About 11 minutes. Answers will vary. Students can show their work on the graph.

5. **A.** Answers will vary. One possible ratio is

$$\frac{90 \text{ calories}}{10 \text{ minutes}}.$$

B. Answers will vary depending on ratio given in 5A. Possible solutions for sample ratio include $\frac{180 \text{ calories}}{20 \text{ minutes}}$ and $\frac{270 \text{ calories}}{30 \text{ minutes}}$.

C. Answers will vary. One possible solution using the answer to *Question 3* is

$$\frac{90 \text{ calories} \times 3}{10 \text{ minutes} \times 3} = \frac{270 \text{ calories}}{30 \text{ minutes}}.$$

Name _____ Date _____

PART 5 Exercising at the Gym
You will need a piece of graph paper to complete this part.

Irma's mother exercises on a stair-step machine for 18 minutes. She exercises at the same rate for the entire time. The following data table shows how many calories she burned at various times.

Time T	Calories Burned C
1	9
5	45
10	90
12	108
18	162

1. Make a point graph of the data on a piece of graph paper. Graph time on the horizontal axis. Be sure to label the axes and to give your graph a title.

2. Use a ruler to fit a line to the points.

3. About how many calories did Irma's mother burn after 15 minutes? How did you decide?

4. About how long did it take her to burn 100 calories? How did you decide?

5. **A.** Choose a point on the graph and use it to write a ratio of calories burned to time taken. (Be sure to include units.)

   B. Write two more ratios equal to the ratio in Question 5A.

   C. If Irma's mother exercised at the same rate for 30 minutes on the stair-step machine, how many calories would she burn? Explain your solution.

FRACTIONS AND RATIOS   DAB • Grade 5 • Unit 3   **29**

Discovery Assignment Book - page 29

---

*Answers for all the Home Practice in the *Discovery Assignment Book* are at the end of the unit.

Name _____ Date _____

Quiz Time

You will need pattern blocks to complete this quiz.

1. **A.** If the blue rhombus is $\frac{1}{2}$, sketch and label one whole.

one-half

B. Which block shows $\frac{1}{4}$?

C. Write a number for 3 purple triangles.

D. Write a number for one yellow hexagon.

2. Show $\frac{2}{3}$ using blue and at least one other color pattern block. The yellow hexagon is one whole. Sketch your figure and write a number sentence for it.

one whole

Copyright © Kendall/Hunt Publishing Company

94   URG • Grade 5 • Unit 3 • Lesson 5   Assessment Blackline Master

Unit Resource Guide - page 94

Unit Resource Guide (p. 94)

Quiz Time

1. **A.** one whole

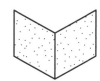

B. green triangle

C. $\frac{3}{8}$

D. $1\frac{1}{2}$

2. Answers will vary. One possible solution is:

$\frac{1}{3} + \frac{1}{6} + \frac{1}{6} = \frac{2}{3}$

Name _____ Date _____

3. **A.** Write $\frac{17}{3}$ as a mixed number.

B. Write $2\frac{5}{6}$ as an improper fraction.

4. Put each of the following sets of fractions in order from smallest to largest.

A. $\frac{7}{8}, \frac{1}{8}, \frac{9}{8}$

B. $\frac{3}{5}, \frac{1}{10}, \frac{4}{9}, \frac{3}{2}$

C. $\frac{1}{2}, \frac{1}{8}, \frac{1}{4}$

5. Complete the following number sentences:

A. $\frac{5}{3} = \frac{?}{12}$

B. $\frac{3}{4} = \frac{15}{?}$

6. Frank wrote the following number sentence: $\frac{20¢}{3 \text{ cookies}} = \frac{10¢}{2 \text{ cookies}}$. Is the number sentence true? Why or why not?

Copyright © Kendall/Hunt Publishing Company

Assessment Blackline Master   URG • Grade 5 • Unit 3 • Lesson 5   95

Unit Resource Guide - page 95

Unit Resource Guide (p. 95)

3. **A.** $5\frac{2}{3}$

B. $\frac{17}{6}$

4. **A.** $\frac{1}{8}, \frac{7}{8}, \frac{9}{8}$

B. $\frac{1}{10}, \frac{4}{9}, \frac{3}{5}, \frac{3}{2}$

C. $\frac{1}{8}, \frac{1}{4}, \frac{1}{2}$

5. **A.** $\frac{5}{3} = \frac{20}{12}$

B. $\frac{3}{4} = \frac{15}{20}$

6. No, $\frac{20¢}{3 \text{ cookies}} = \frac{10¢}{1\frac{1}{2} \text{ cookies}}$ or $\frac{10¢}{2 \text{ cookies}} = \frac{20¢}{4 \text{ cookies}}$

Unit Resource Guide (p. 96)

7.

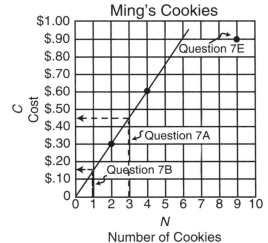

Ming's Cookies

A. $.45
B. $.15
C. $\frac{\$.90}{6 \text{ cookies}}$
D. 20 cookies
E. No; $\frac{\$.90}{9 \text{ cookies}} = \frac{\$.10}{1 \text{ cookie}}$

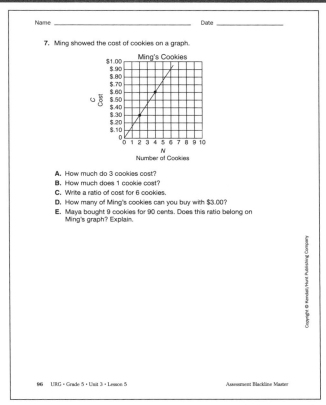

Name _____   Date _____

7. Ming showed the cost of cookies on a graph.

Ming's Cookies

A. How much do 3 cookies cost?
B. How much does 1 cookie cost?
C. Write a ratio of cost for 6 cookies.
D. How many of Ming's cookies can you buy with $3.00?
E. Maya bought 9 cookies for 90 cents. Does this ratio belong on Ming's graph? Explain.

96   URG • Grade 5 • Unit 3 • Lesson 5   Assessment Blackline Master

Unit Resource Guide - **page 96**

Lesson 6

Distance vs. Time

Estimated Class Sessions

4

Lesson Overview

Using the TIMS Laboratory Method, students investigate the walking speed of a classmate. They review measuring length, plotting points, and drawing best-fit lines. In the final section, students use ratios to solve problems.

Key Content

- Using numerical variables.
- Measuring length in yards and feet.
- Averaging: finding the median.
- Drawing and interpreting best-fit lines.
- Collecting, organizing, graphing, and analyzing data.
- Using ratios to solve problems.
- Using patterns in data to solve problems.
- Translating between graphs and real-world events.

Key Vocabulary

- best-fit line
- fixed variable
- speed

Math Facts

Review the multiplication and division facts for the 2s and 3s. Complete DPP item O.

Homework

1. Assign the Homework section in the *Student Guide*.
2. Assign the problems in Lesson 7 *Speedy Problems*.

Assessment

1. Use DPP item U to assess students' fluency with the multiplication and division facts for the 2s and 3s.
2. Use the *Observational Assessment Record* and the *Individual Assessment Record Sheet* as you observe students measuring length.
3. Assess students' graphing abilities by scoring their graphs.
4. Use the rubrics *Knowing* and *Telling* to assess students' work on **Questions 16–18** in the Explore section.
5. Use DPP item V to assess ratio concepts.

Curriculum Sequence

Before This Unit

TIMS Laboratory Method

Students reviewed the TIMS Laboratory Method in Unit 1 by completing two labs, *Eyelets* and *Searching the Forest.*

Best-Fit Lines

Students learned to plot points and draw best-fit lines in third grade. In fourth grade, they continued to graph data, decide if the points suggested a line, and fit a line to the data points. See the fourth-grade labs *Bouncing Ball* in Unit 5, *Volume vs. Number* in Unit 8, and *Downhill Racer* in Unit 10.

After This Unit

TIMS Laboratory Method and Best-Fit Lines

In fifth grade, students complete a series of labs in which they collect data and graph points that lie close to a straight line. They draw best-fit lines and use the lines to find ratios and solve problems involving proportional reasoning. These labs include: *Spreading*

Out in Unit 4, *A Day at the Races* in Unit 5, *Mass vs. Volume* in Unit 13, *Circumference vs. Diameter* in Unit 14, and the assessment lab *Bats* in Unit 16. In the lab *A Day at the Races,* students again graph distance vs. time to compare the speeds of runners, walkers, hoppers, etc. In the lab *Mass vs. Volume,* they use the line to find the ratio of mass/volume (density) of steel and plastic.

Materials List

Supplies and Copies

Student	Teacher
Supplies for Each Student • chalk or tape • calculator **Supplies for Each Student Group** • 3 stopwatches • 1–2 metersticks	**Supplies**
Copies • 1 copy of *Using Best-Fit Lines* per student, optional (*Unit Resource Guide* Pages 126–131) • 1 copy of *Centimeter Graph Paper* per student (*Unit Resource Guide* Page 100) • 1 copy of *Three-trial Data Table* per student (*Unit Resource Guide* Page 132)	**Copies/Transparencies** • 1 transparency of *Nila's Sit-Ups*, optional (*Unit Resource Guide* Page 124) • 1 transparency of *What's Wrong with This Graph?*, optional (*Unit Resource Guide* Page 125) • 1 transparency of *Centimeter Graph Paper*, optional (*Unit Resource Guide* Page 100) • 1 transparency or wall chart of Student Rubric: *Knowing* (*Teacher Implementation Guide*, Assessment section) • 1 transparency or wall chart of Student Rubric: *Telling* (*Teacher Implementation Guide*, Assessment section) • 1 copy of *TIMS Multidimensional Rubric* (*Teacher Implementation Guide*, Assessment section) • 1 copy of *Observational Assessment Record* to be used throughout this unit (*Unit Resource Guide* Pages 11–12)

All blackline masters including assessment, transparency, and DPP masters are also on the Teacher Resource CD.

Student Books
Distance vs. Time (*Student Guide* Pages 94–98)
Student Rubric: *Knowing* (*Student Guide* Appendix A and Inside Back Cover)
Student Rubric: *Telling* (*Student Guide* Appendix C and Inside Back Cover)

Daily Practice and Problems and Home Practice
DPP items O–V (*Unit Resource Guide* Pages 24–30)

Note: Classrooms whose pacing differs significantly from the suggested pacing of the units should use the Math Facts Calendar in Section 4 of the *Facts Resource Guide* to ensure students receive the complete math facts program.

Assessment Tools
Observational Assessment Record (*Unit Resource Guide* Pages 11–12)
Individual Assessment Record Sheet (*Teacher Implementation Guide*, Assessment section)
TIMS Multidimensional Rubric (*Teacher Implementation Guide*, Assessment section)

Daily Practice and Problems

Suggestions for using the DPPs are on pages 120–121.

O. Bit: Fact Families for × and ÷
(URG p. 24)

Complete the number sentences for the related facts.

A. $3 \times 10 =$ ____

    ____ ÷ 3 = ____

    ____ ÷ 10 = ____

    ____ × 3 = ____

B. $3 \times 7 =$ ____

    ____ ÷ 7 = ____

    ____ ÷ 3 = ____

    7 × ____ = ____

C. $2 \times 2 =$ ____

    ____ ÷ 2 = ____

D. $12 ÷ 6 =$ ____

    ____ × 6 = ____

    12 ÷ ____ = ____

    ____ × 2 = ____

E. $3 \times$ ____ $= 9$

    9 ÷ ____ = ____

P. Task: Trading Times (URG p. 25)

Use the following information to answer the questions below. Check to see if your answers are reasonable.

60 seconds = 1 minute   24 hours = 1 day
60 minutes = 1 hour   7 days = 1 week

1. 10 days = ? hours
2. 5 weeks = ? days
3. 20 hours = ? minutes
4. 30 minutes = ? seconds
5. $3\frac{1}{2}$ hours = ? minutes
6. 56 days = ? weeks

Q. Bit: Comparing Fractions (URG p. 25)

Which fractions below are:

$\frac{3}{5}$ $\frac{1}{10}$ $\frac{2}{4}$ $\frac{9}{8}$ $\frac{1}{3}$ $\frac{4}{5}$ $\frac{3}{6}$ $\frac{8}{12}$ $\frac{2}{6}$

1. Equal to $\frac{1}{2}$?
2. Less than $\frac{1}{2}$?
3. Greater than $\frac{1}{2}$?

R. Task: What's My Length?
(URG p. 26)

1. A. How many inches are in one foot?
    B. How many inches are in 5 feet?
    C. Name something that is about 1 inch long.
    D. Name something that is about 1 foot long.
2. A. How many feet are in one yard?
    B. How many yards is 24 feet?
    C. How many feet are in 6 yards?
    D. Name something that is about 1 yard long.
3. Which is longer, a yardstick or a meterstick? How much longer?

S. Bit: Choosing Units of Measure
(URG p. 27)

The following are some units of measure for length: meters, centimeters, feet, inches, yards, kilometers, and miles.

Which unit of measure does it make sense to use when you measure:

1. the length of a book?
2. the distance from your classroom door to your teacher's desk?
3. the distance from your home to school?
4. a person's height?

Daily Practice and Problems

Suggestions for using the DPPs are on pages 120–121.

T. Task: Subtracting Time (URG p. 28)

Jerome is traveling on a train. He is going to visit his aunt. The train ride is 4 hours and 30 minutes long. So far he has traveled for 2 hours and 45 minutes. Jerome wants to know how much longer the train ride is. He writes the following:

4 hours 30 minutes	3 hours 90 minutes
−2 hours 45 minutes	−2 hours 45 minutes
	1 hour 45 minutes

Jerome still has 1 hour and 45 minutes left on his train ride.

1. Explain how Jerome changed 4 hours 30 minutes to 3 hours and 90 minutes. Why did he rewrite the problem?

2. Solve these problems.
   A. 7 hours 18 minutes − 4 hours 16 minutes
   B. 5 hours 26 minutes − 2 hours 36 minutes
   C. 12 hours 28 minutes − 6 hours 54 minutes
   D. 17 hours 47 minutes − 6 hours 50 minutes

U. Bit: Quiz: 2s and 3s (URG p. 29)

A. $3 \times 5 =$ B. $14 \div 2 =$
C. $18 \div 3 =$ D. $3 \times 10 =$
E. $2 \times 2 =$ F. $7 \times 3 =$
G. $12 \div 6 =$ H. $8 \div 4 =$
I. $12 \div 4 =$ J. $24 \div 3 =$
K. $9 \div 3 =$ L. $2 \times 9 =$
M. $9 \times 3 =$ N. $5 \times 2 =$
O. $16 \div 8 =$ P. $3 \times 2 =$
Q. $20 \div 2 =$

V. Task: Goldfish on Sale (URG p. 30)

1. Complete the table for the cost of fancy goldfish.

N Number of Goldfish	C Cost
2	$3.00
4	
	$7.50

2. Using fractions, write three other ratios that are equal to $\frac{\$3.00}{2 \text{ fish}}$.

3. How much will 3 dozen fancy goldfish cost?

Students new to *Math Trailblazers* may need to learn to fit a line to a set of points on a graph and to use the line to make predictions. The *Using Best-Fit Lines* Activity Pages are taken from a fourth grade unit (Unit 5 *Using Data to Predict*) and are included at the end of this Lesson Guide for these students. On the *Using Best-Fit Lines* Activity Pages, students find six different point graphs. For each graph, they describe any patterns they see in the data. Encourage students to describe patterns in terms of lines or curves. Do the points tend to go uphill or downhill? If the points suggest a line, students should draw a best-fit line. A transparency master of the graph in *Question 1* is provided so you can model drawing a best-fit line using a ruler. See Figure 11.

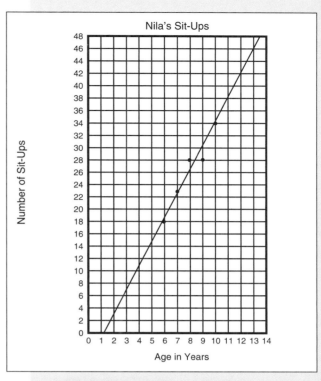

Figure 11: *Drawing a best-fit line*

Content Note

Best-fit Lines. A **best-fit line** is the line that comes closest to the most number of points. To fit a line, try to get as many points above the line as below it. Students use a ruler (preferably clear) to experiment with the various angles, then draw it using a pencil. (Students can also experiment with a piece of string or spaghetti, but they should use a ruler to draw the line.) Each student will draw the line a little differently and use it to make predictions. This will result in differing predictions. However, you can expect the lines and predictions to be relatively close. For more information, see the TIMS Tutor: *The TIMS Laboratory Method* in the *Teacher Implementation Guide.*

The points on the graph in *Question 2* do suggest a line. Students should see, however, that extrapolating far beyond the last data point is not reliable. According to the graph, John will run the mile in one minute when he is 18 years old *(Question 2E).* This is impossible. The points on the graph in *Question 3* do not form a line or any particular pattern since there is little relationship between the number of letters in a person's name and the month that person was born. It would not make sense to try to draw a line or to make a prediction using the graph. The points in the graph in *Question 5* do not suggest a line, but they do form a curve. Even though it would not make sense to draw a best-fit line, it is possible to use the graph to predict the head circumference of a baby if you know the baby's age.

TIMS Tip

If you have a few students who are new to *Math Trailblazers,* pair them with students who drew best-fit lines in fourth grade and the experienced students can serve as peer tutors.

Read and discuss *Questions 1–3* at the beginning of the *Distance vs. Time* Lab Pages in the *Student Guide.* These questions provide the context for the lab. They ask students to estimate how far they can

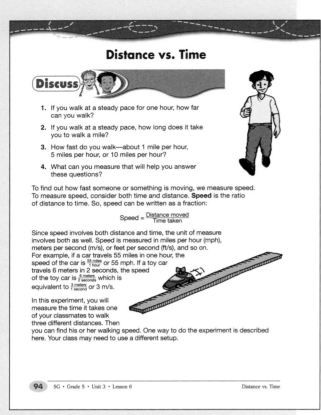

Student Guide - page 94 *(Answers on p. 133)*

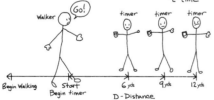

Student Guide - page 95 *(Answers on p. 133)*

walk in one hour, how long it takes them to walk a mile, and how fast they walk.

Question 4 asks students what they will measure during the lab. To help them answer this question, they can read and discuss the definition of speed and the description of the experiment. **Speed** is defined as the ratio of the distance moved to the time taken. In the experiment, students measure the time it takes for a fifth grader to walk three given distances and use the data to find the walker's speed.

TIMS Tip

To encourage class participation, ask students to discuss their thinking with a partner or small group before they report their answers to the whole class.

Part 1 Setting Up the Lab and Drawing the Picture

The directions in the *Student Guide* advise students to measure out a track that is 12 yards long and to mark distances on the track that are 6, 9, and 12 yards from the starting line. (See the diagram in the *Student Guide*.) These distances are the minimum distances students should use. If the distances are shorter, they probably cannot stop the watches fast enough to collect accurate data. However, if you can conduct the lab outside on a playground, in a gym, or in a hallway, the distances can be longer. Encourage students to choose values which are all multiples of one number (6, 9, and 12 yards are all multiples of 3), so that they can more readily see patterns in the data table.

One student in each group is designated the "walker." He or she begins walking at a steady rate several paces behind the starting line. When the walker crosses the starting line, he or she says, "Go," and timers stationed at each distance marked on the track start their stopwatches. When the walker crosses each mark, the timer at that distance stops his or her watch.

The following questions can be used to lead a class discussion about the variables in the lab?

- *What variables will you measure in the lab?* *(Question 6A)* (time and distance)

- *What symbols will you use to stand for distance and time?* (D and T)

- *What variables should be held fixed?* *(Question 6B)* (The walker should walk at the same pace throughout the experiment, and the timers should stop their watches when the walker's front foot touches or crosses their marks.)

- *Why should the walker begin walking several paces behind the starting line?* (He or she will be walking at a steady pace when the starting line is reached.)
- *Why is it a good idea to record the results of three trials and average the results?* (Averaging the results of three trials reduces the effects of experimental error. If the time for one trial is not close to the other two trials, then the trial should be repeated.)

If the setup in your classroom is different from the setup in the diagram in the *Student Guide,* then students should draw pictures of their setup. Remind them to clearly show in their pictures the variables they will study.

Part 2 Collecting the Data

Each group should practice using the stopwatches and timing the walker. When the timers are proficient with the stopwatches and the walker can walk at a constant speed, they are ready to collect the data. They repeat the procedure three times and record each trial in a *Three-trial Data Table* as shown in Figure 12. In each table, the results for the three trials are averaged (using the median), rounded to the nearest second, and recorded in the last column. The data tables in Figure 12 show the median rounded to the nearest second.

> ## TIMS Tip
>
> Students may need to practice using the stopwatches before they collect data. DPP item J provides such an opportunity.

> ## TIMS Tip
>
> If all the groups cannot collect data at one time, students can work on the problems in Lesson 7 or DPP items P, R, and V while other students are collecting data.

Part 3 Graphing the Data

Students make a point graph of the data. In this experiment distance (*D*) is the manipulated variable and time (*T*) is the responding variable. However, scientists usually graph time on the horizontal axis. So students should graph *T* on the horizontal axis and *D* on the vertical axis (see content note). *Question 9* asks students to give the measurements for time and

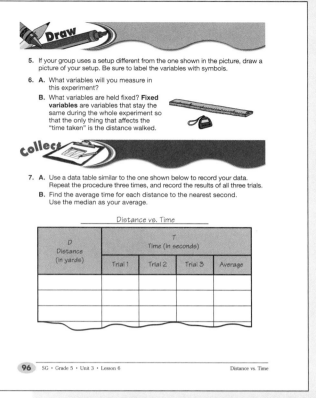

Student Guide - page 96 (Answers on p. 133)

Sample Data Table A

D Distance (in yards)	T Time (in seconds)			
	Trial 1	Trial 2	Trial 3	Average
6	4.50	3.88	4.34	4
9	6.75	6.31	6.40	6
12	8.50	8.25	8.35	8

Sample Data Table B

D Distance (in yards)	T Time (in seconds)			
	Trial 1	Trial 2	Trial 3	Average
6	3.23	3.40	4.22	3
9	5.75	5.00	6.19	6
12	7.63	7.04	9.07	8

Figure 12: *Sample data tables*

8. Make a point graph of your data. Scientists usually graph time (*T*) on the horizontal axis and distance (*D*) on the vertical axis.

9. What were the measurements for time and distance when the walker crossed the starting line? (When *D* = 0 yds, *T* = ? sec.) Add this point to your graph.

10. If your points lie close to a line, use a ruler to draw a best-fit line. The **best-fit line** is the line that comes closest to the most number of points.

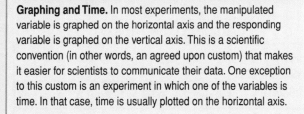

11. Use your graph to find the time taken to walk 8 yards.

12. Find the distance walked after 10 seconds.
    A. Give your answer in yards.
    B. Give your answer in feet.

13. A. Choose a point on the line. Use it to write the walker's speed as a ratio of distance traveled to time taken written as a fraction.
    B. Write two more ratios equal to the ratio in Part A.

14. A. How many yards did the walker travel in one second?
    B. Give the walker's speed in yards per second (yd/s).

15. A. How many feet does the walker travel in one second?
    B. Give the walker's speed in feet per second (ft/s).

16. A. If the walker continues at the same pace for one hour, about how far will he or she walk? Explain how you found your answer.
    B. About how many miles can he or she walk in one hour? (1 mile = 5280 ft) Check your answer. Is it reasonable?

Distance vs. Time   SG • Grade 5 • Unit 3 • Lesson 6   **97**

Student Guide - page 97 *(Answers on p. 134)*

Content Note

Graphing and Time. In most experiments, the manipulated variable is graphed on the horizontal axis and the responding variable is graphed on the vertical axis. This is a scientific convention (in other words, an agreed upon custom) that makes it easier for scientists to communicate their data. One exception to this custom is an experiment in which one of the variables is time. In that case, time is usually plotted on the horizontal axis.

distance when the walker crosses the starting line and to add this point to their graphs. When the walker crosses the starting line, the distance traveled is 0 yards and the stopwatches should all read 0 seconds. Students should use a ruler to fit a line through all four points *(Question 10)*.

To emphasize the important items in graphing the data, show the class the transparency *What's Wrong with This Graph?* Students should see the following mistakes in the graph: Time and distance are graphed on the wrong axes; the point for 0 sec, 0 yds has not been added to the graph, so the best-fit line does not go through (0,0); and the graph has no title. Figure 13 provides sample graphs corresponding to the data tables in Figure 12.

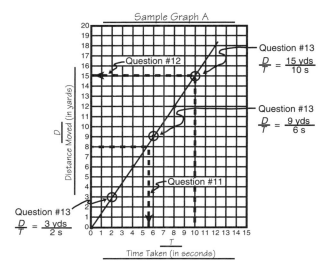

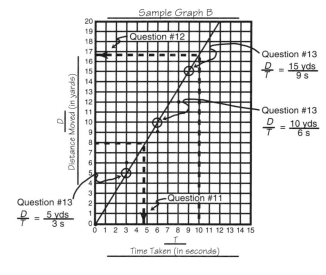

Figure 13: *Sample graphs A and B*

Note that the four data points plotted on sample Graph A lie directly on a straight line, so the best-fit line goes through all four points. However, since the four points on sample Graph B suggest a linear pattern but do not fall exactly on a line, the best-fit line in Graph B goes through (0,0) but falls between the other three points. It is likely that different groups will produce different graphs.

Part 4 Exploring the Data

Figure 13 illustrates how students can use their graphs to answer *Questions 11–12A.* (Note that the graphs give slightly different answers.) *Question 13* asks students to choose a point from the graph and write the walker's speed as a ratio of distance to time ($\frac{D}{T}$) and then write two more equal ratios as fractions. The three points used to write the ratios are circled on each graph in Figure 13. They are written below as fractions:

$$\text{Graph A: } \frac{D}{T} = \frac{3 \text{ yds}}{2 \text{ s}} = \frac{9 \text{ yds}}{6 \text{ s}} = \frac{15 \text{ yds}}{10 \text{ s}}$$

$$\text{Graph B: } \frac{D}{T} = \frac{5 \text{ yds}}{3 \text{ s}} = \frac{10 \text{ yds}}{6 \text{ s}} = \frac{15 \text{ yds}}{9 \text{ s}}$$

If the line goes through (0 sec, 0 yds), the three ratios should be equal. There may be some error due to errors in estimating the values of the coordinates when reading the graph. However, all three ratios should be very close. If not, check to see that the line goes through (0 sec, 0 yds) and students choose points on intersections to find the ratio.

Question 14 asks for the walker's speed in yards per second. Using Graph A, we can estimate the distance traveled in one second to be 1.5 yards. Note that the ratio $\frac{D}{T} = \frac{3 \text{ yd}}{2 \text{ s}}$ can also be written as $\frac{1.5 \text{ yd}}{1 \text{ s}}$ or 1.5 yd/s. Using this information, we can calculate the walker's speed in feet per second by multiplying the number of yards walked in one second by 3 (3 ft = 1 yd), so the walker's speed is 4.5 ft/s *(Question 15)*.

TIMS Tip

Students should use their own data tables and graphs to answer the remaining questions. In this lab, it is possible that a group did not use the stopwatches correctly or the walker didn't walk at a steady pace. These errors would probably result in data points that do not fall close to a straight line. In that case, groups can share their data or the class can use the most reasonable data set to complete the lab.

Content Note

Equal Ratios and Graphs. *Question 13* emphasizes an important concept: When equal ratios are plotted on a coordinate grid, they form a straight line through (0,0). This concept is used extensively throughout the curriculum as one tool for solving problems involving proportional reasoning. For example, students can answer *Questions 11–12* by using their graphs, as shown in Figure 13. They can also solve the problems by finding equivalent fractions for the ratios. When students can use more than one method, they can also make connections between the graphical and symbolic representation of the ratios.

There are many possible strategies for solving **Questions 16–17.** Students may use calculators to multiply and divide the large numbers in the problems or estimate by multiplying and dividing convenient numbers. One way to solve **Question 16A** is to multiply the number of feet walked in one second by 3600 seconds (the number of seconds in one hour). The following number sentences show calculations with a calculator and with convenient numbers:

Using a calculator:
4.5 ft/s $\times$ 3600 s $=$ 16,200 ft/hr

Using convenient numbers:
4 ft/s $\times$ 4000 s $\approx$ 16,000 ft/hr

Since 4.5 is midway between 4 and 5 and 3600 is about midway between 3000 and 4000, we choose to round 4.5 down to 4 and 3600 up to 4000 so the product is a pretty good estimate.

To estimate the number of miles the walker can walk in one hour **(Question 16B),** students can divide the number of feet he or she can walk in one hour by 5280 ft as shown here:

Using a calculator:
16,200 ft/hr $\div$ 5280 ft $=$ 3.0681818 mi or about 3 mi

Using convenient numbers:
15,000 ft/hr $\div$ 5000 ft $\approx$ 3 mi

To answer **Question 17**, students may reason as follows: The walker can walk 3 miles in one hour, so it will take him $\frac{1}{3}$ hour or 20 minutes to walk one mile.

Since both the data and problem-solving strategies will vary from student group to student group, solutions will vary also. To know if students calculated correctly, it is necessary for them to describe their choices and their problem-solving process clearly.

Math Facts

DPP item O provides practice with fact families for the 2s and 3s.

Homework and Practice

- Assign the Homework section in the *Student Guide.*
- Assign the problems in Lesson 7 *Speedy Problems.*
- DPP Tasks P and T include problems on elapsed time. DPP Bit Q provides practice comparing fractions. DPP items R and S review length measurement.

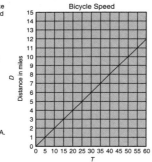

17. If the walker continues at the same pace, about how long will it take him or her to walk one mile?

18. Do you think the walker can walk at the same speed you calculated in Questions 16 and 17 for one hour or longer? Why or why not?

Homework

Felicia biked for one hour on a bike path. She biked at the same speed for the entire time. The following graph shows her speed.

1. How far did Felicia travel after 15 minutes?

2. How long did it take Felicia to bike 10 miles?

3. A. Choose a point on the graph. Use it to write Felicia's speed as a ratio of distance traveled to time taken. (Include units.)

  B. Write two more ratios equal to the ratio in Part A.

Bicycle Speed

Distance in miles

Time in minutes

4. If Felicia biked at the same speed for $1\frac{1}{2}$ hours, how far would she travel? Explain how you know.

5. The bike path is 16 miles long. If Felicia biked the entire path at the same speed, how long did she travel? Explain how you know.

6. A. How far did Felicia travel in one hour?

  B. Give Felicia's speed in miles per hour.

Student Guide - page 98 *(Answers on p. 135)*

- Use DPP item U to assess students' fluency with the multiplication and division facts for the 2s and 3s.

- Use the *Observational Assessment Record* in the *Unit Resource Guide* and the *Individual Assessment Record Sheet* in the *Teacher Implementation Guide* to record student success in measuring length in yards as students measure the track for the lab.

- Assess students' abilities to use a point graph to recognize a straight line pattern in data and use a best-fit line to make predictions. Record student achievement on the *Observational Assessment Record.* Or, assign points to different parts of the graph and a score for the entire graph. Check for the following:

  1. Does the graph have a title?

  2. Did the student graph time on the horizontal axis and distance on the vertical axis?

  3. Are the axes labeled with the appropriate variables and units of measure?

  4. Are the axes scaled correctly?

  5. Are the points plotted correctly? Did the student add a point at (0 sec, 0 yds)?

  6. Did the student use a ruler to draw an accurate best-fit line?

  7. Did the student correctly use the line to answer **Questions 11–12?**

  8. Did the student choose a grid point on the line to accurately write the ratio of distance moved to time taken in **Question 13?**

- Advise students that you will use the *Student Rubrics: Knowing* and *Telling* to score their answers to **Questions 16–18.** Ask them to review the student rubrics. As students write and revise, encourage them to use correct number sentences and to explain what each number refers to in each sentence. They should also be able to describe why their method makes sense. Then score their responses using the appropriate dimensions of the *TIMS Multidimensional Rubric* in the Assessment section of the *Teacher Implementation Guide.*

- Use DPP item V to assess students' understanding of equal ratios.

Journal Prompt

How do you measure speed?

At a Glance

Math Facts and Daily Practice and Problems

Review the multiplication and division facts for the 2s and 3s. Complete DPP items O–V.

Before the Lab

For students who do not know how to draw a best-fit line for points plotted on a graph, use the *Using Best-Fit Lines* Activity Pages at the end of the Lesson Guide.

Part 1. Setting Up the Lab and Drawing the Picture

1. Use *Questions 1–3* on the *Distance vs. Time Lab* Pages in the *Student Guide* to set the context for the lab.
2. Discuss the variables involved in the lab using *Questions 4–6* in the *Student Guide* and discussion prompts in the Lesson Guide.
3. Students measure tracks 12 yards long. Following the diagram in the *Student Guide,* they mark distances at 6, 9, and 12 yards from the starting line.
4. Students draw a picture of the experimental setup if it differs from the diagram in the *Student Guide.*

Part 2. Collecting the Data

1. Students collect the data in groups. One student is the walker; three students are timers. They record the time the walker travels 6, 9, and 12 yards. They repeat the procedure 3 times for each distance and record the times in a *Three-trial Data Table. (Question 7)*
2. Students find the average time (the median) for each trial and record it in the data table.

Part 3. Graphing the Data

1. Students make a point graph of the data. *(Question 8)*
2. Students add the point (0 sec, 0 yds) to their graphs. This point corresponds to the time on the stopwatches when the walker is at the starting line. *(Question 9)*
3. They use a ruler to fit a line to the four data points. *(Question 10)*

Part 4. Exploring the Data

1. Students use their graphs to answer *Questions 11–13.*
2. Solving the remaining problems will help students find answers to the questions posed at the beginning of the lesson. *(Questions 14–18)*

Homework

1. Assign the Homework section in the *Student Guide.*
2. Assign the problems in Lesson 7 *Speedy Problems.*

At a Glance

1. Use DPP item U to assess students' fluency with the multiplication and division facts for the 2s and 3s.
2. Use the *Observational Assessment Record* and the *Individual Assessment Record Sheet* as you observe students measuring length.
3. Assess students' graphing abilities by scoring their graphs.
4. Use the rubrics *Knowing* and *Telling* to assess students' work on **Questions 16–18** in the Explore section.
5. Use DPP item V to assess ratio concepts.

Answer Key is on pages 133–139.

Notes:

Nila's Sit-Ups

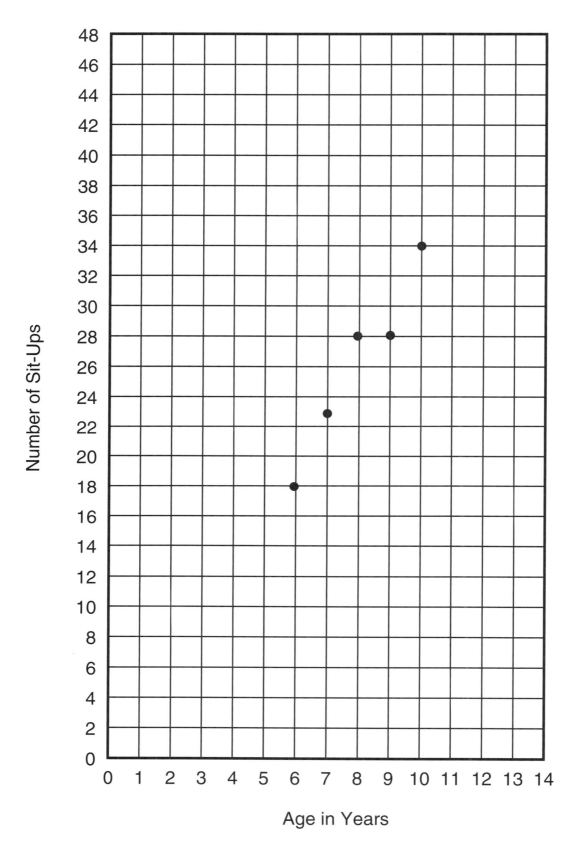

Age in Years

Transparency Master

What's Wrong with This Graph?

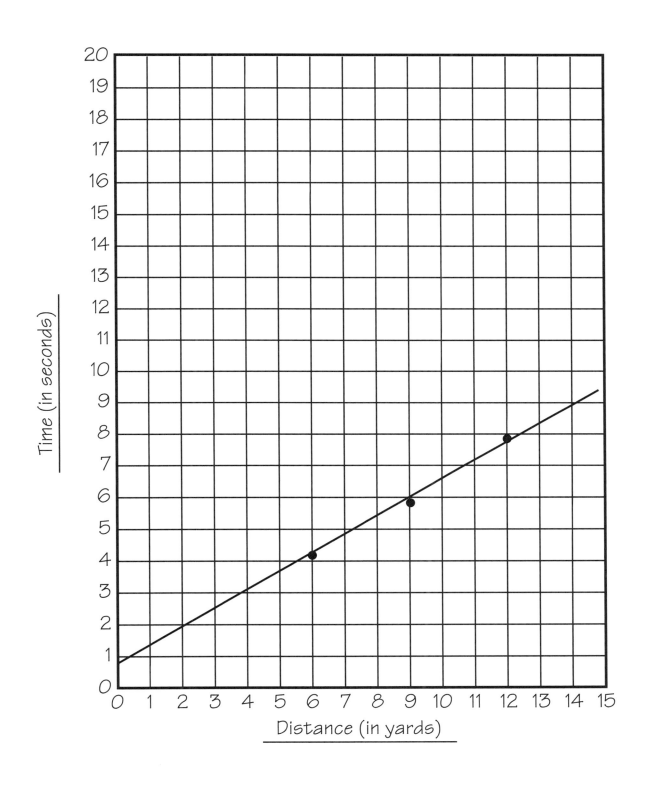

Using Best-Fit Lines

1. Each year, Mrs. Welch, a gym teacher at Bessie Coleman School, records the number of sit-ups each student can do. Nila used her data to make a graph showing the number of sit-ups she could do each year.

   A. Describe the graph.

   B. If you read the graph from left to right, do the points go uphill or downhill?

   C. What does the graph tell you about the number of sit-ups Nila can do?

   D. Do the points lie close to a straight line? If so, use a ruler to draw a best-fit line.

   E. If possible, predict the number of sit-ups Nila will be able to do when she is 12.

   F. Does knowing Nila's age help you predict the number of sit-ups she can do?

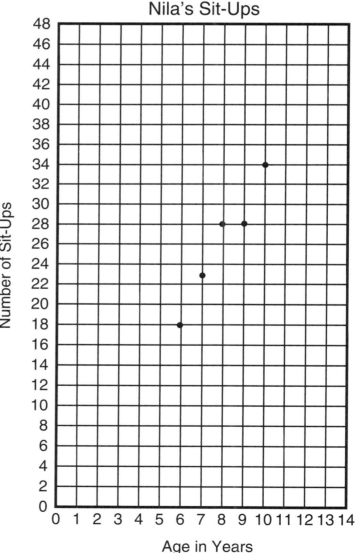

Nila's Sit-Ups

Number of Sit-Ups

Age in Years

Blackline Master

2. Mrs. Welch also records each student's best times for running a mile. John graphed his best times.

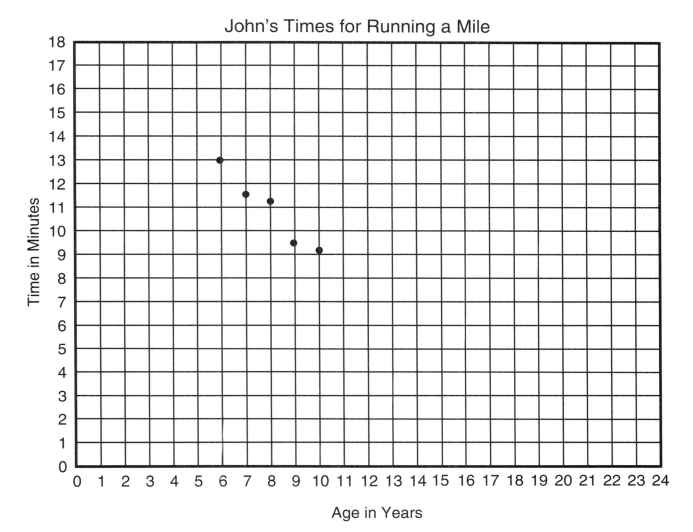

A. Describe the graph.

B. Do the points tend to go uphill or downhill as you read the graph from left to right?

C. Do the points lie close to a straight line? If so, use a ruler to draw a best-fit line.

D. If possible, predict how long it will take John to run a mile when he is 12.

E. If possible, predict how long it will take John to run a mile when he is 18.

F. Does knowing John's age help you predict his time for running the mile?

3. A fourth-grade class recorded the month each student was born and the number of letters in each student's name. Using the data, the class made the following graph.

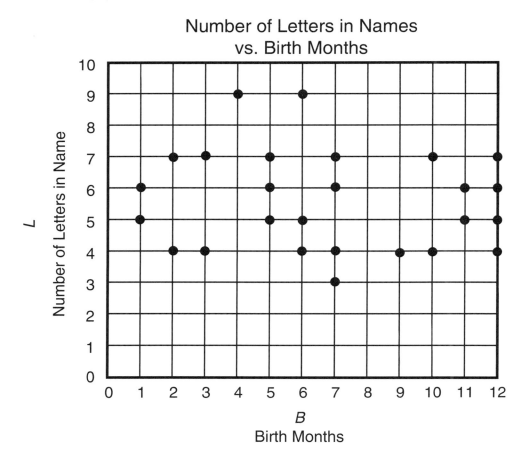

Number of Letters in Names vs. Birth Months

A. Describe the graph.

B. Do the points lie close to a straight line? If so, use a ruler to draw a best-fit line.

C. Does knowing the month a student was born help you predict the number of letters in his or her name?

D. If possible, predict the number of letters in a student's name if he or she was born in August (the eighth month).

4. A cookie company wants all the cookies from the factory to be the same. Here is a graph made by a cookie inspector.

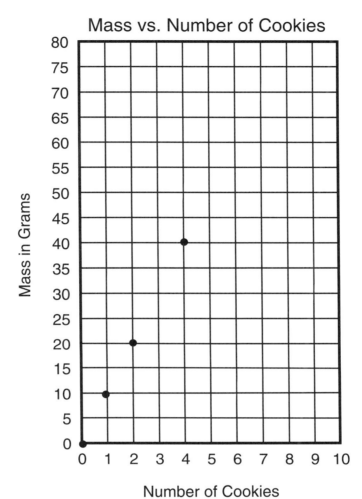

Mass vs. Number of Cookies

A. Describe the graph.

B. Do the points lie close to a straight line? If so, use a ruler to draw a best-fit line.

C. If possible, predict the mass of 3 cookies.

D. If possible, predict the mass of 5 cookies.

5. Doctors measure the head circumference of babies to track their growth.

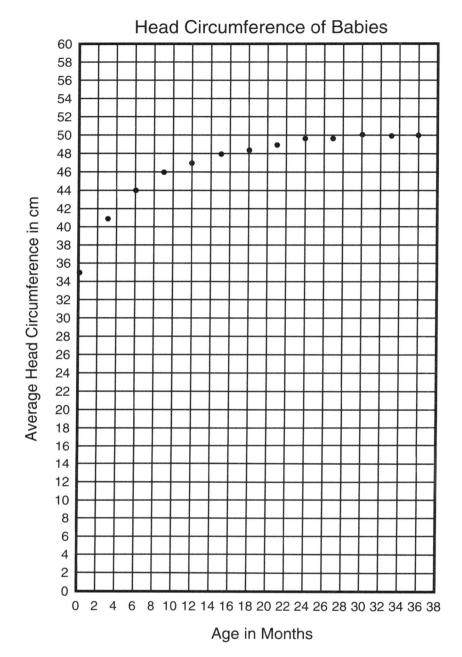

A. Describe the graph.

B. If the points lie close to a line, use a ruler to draw a best-fit line.

C. If possible, predict the head circumference of a baby who is four years old.

6. The winning times for the women's Olympic breaststroke swimming competition are shown in this graph.

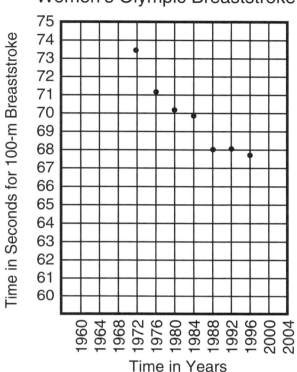

Winning Times for the Women's Olympic Breaststroke

A. Describe the graph.

B. If the points lie close to a line, use a ruler to draw a best-fit line.

7. Look back at the graphs in Questions 1–6. Which graph gives the most accurate predictions? Explain your choice

Name _____ Date _____

_____

		Trial 1	Trial 2	Trial 3	Average

Three-trial Data Table, Blackline Master

Student Guide (pp. 94–96)

Distance vs. Time

1.–3. Estimates will vary. Ask students to explain how they arrived at their estimates.

4. speed (distance moved and time taken)

5. A sample picture is provided in the *Student Guide.* If your class uses a different setup, check that students' pictures accurately describe the setup. Make sure the variables are labeled.

6. A. distance and time

B. The walker should walk at the same pace throughout the experiment. The timers should stop their watches when the walker's front foot touches or crosses their marks.

7. See Figure 12 in Lesson Guide 6 for sample data.

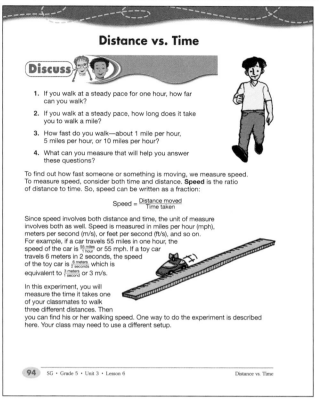

Student Guide - page 94

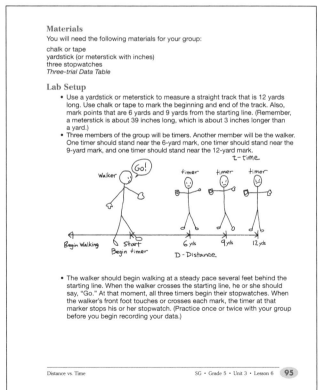

Student Guide - page 95

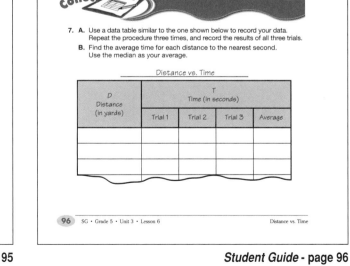

Student Guide - page 96

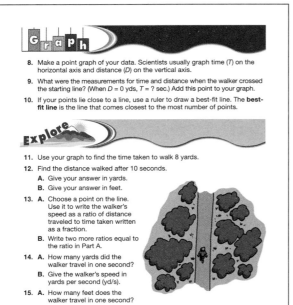

Student Guide - page 97

Student Guide (p. 97)

8.–10. See Figure 13 in Lesson Guide 6 for sample graphs.

The answers to **Questions 11–18** will vary. Those provided here are based on Sample Data Tables A and B and Sample Graphs A and B in Figures 12 and 13 in Lesson Guide 6.

11. Sample Graph A: $5\frac{1}{2}$ seconds;

Sample Graph B: $4\frac{2}{3}$ seconds*

12. A. Sample Graph A: 15 yards;

Sample Graph B: $16\frac{2}{3}$ yards*

B. Sample Graph A: 45 feet;
Sample Graph B: 50 feet

13. A. Sample Graph A: $\frac{D}{T} = \frac{3\text{ yds.}}{2\text{ s}}$;

Graph B: $\frac{D}{T} = \frac{5\text{ yds.}}{3\text{ s}}$*

B. Sample Graph A: $\frac{D}{T} = \frac{15\text{ yds.}}{10\text{s}}, \frac{D}{T} = \frac{9\text{ yds.}}{6\text{ s}}$,

Graph B: $\frac{D}{T} = \frac{15\text{ yds.}}{9\text{ s}}, \frac{D}{T} = \frac{10\text{ yds}}{6\text{ s}}$

14.* A. Sample Graph A: 1.5 yards;

Sample Graph B: $1\frac{2}{3}$ yards

B. Sample Graph A: 1.5 yd/s;
Sample Graph B: 1.67 yd/s

15.* A. Sample Graph A: 4.5 feet;
Sample Graph B: 5 feet

B. Sample Graph A: 4.5 ft/s;
Sample Graph B: 5 ft/s

16.* A. Sample Graph A: 16,200 feet or 5400 yards;
Sample Graph B: about 18,000 feet or about 6000 yards

B. *Sample Graph A: About 3 miles.
Sample Graph B: Between 3 and 4 miles.

*Answers and/or discussion are included in the Lesson Guide.

Student Guide (p. 98)

17. About 20 minutes.*

18. Answers will vary. No. The walker may get tired. If his or her path goes uphill, the walker may slow down.

Homework

1. 3 miles

2. 50 minutes

3. A. Answers will vary. One possible ratio is:

$$\frac{1 \text{ mile}}{5 \text{ minutes}} .$$

B. Answers will vary. Two possible ratios are:

$$\frac{2 \text{ miles}}{10 \text{ minutes}} \text{ and } \frac{3 \text{ miles}}{15 \text{ minutes}} .$$

4. 18 miles, strategies will vary. Students might find out how far Felicia can bike in 1 hour (12 miles), then take half (6 miles) and add it on.

5. 80 minutes or 1 hour and 20 minutes. Strategies will vary. Students can double the time it takes her to travel 8 miles.

6. A. 12 miles

B. 12 miles per hour

17. If the walker continues at the same pace, about how long will it take him or her to walk one mile?

18. Do you think the walker can walk at the same speed you calculated in Questions 16 and 17 for one hour or longer? Why or why not?

Homework

Felicia biked for one hour on a bike path. She biked at the same speed for the entire time. The following graph shows her speed.

1. How far did Felicia travel after 15 minutes?

2. How long did it take Felicia to bike 10 miles?

3. A. Choose a point on the graph. Use it to write Felicia's speed as a ratio of distance traveled to time taken. (Include units.)

B. Write two more ratios equal to the ratio in Part A.

4. If Felicia biked at the same speed for $1\frac{1}{2}$ hours, how far would she travel? Explain how you know.

5. The bike path is 16 miles long. If Felicia biked the entire path at the same speed, how long did she travel? Explain how you know.

6. A. How far did Felicia travel in one hour?

B. Give Felicia's speed in miles per hour.

98 SG • Grade 5 • Unit 3 • Lesson 6   Distance vs. Time

Student Guide - page 98

*Answers and/or discussion are included in the Lesson Guide.

Using Best-Fit Lines

1. Each year, Mrs. Welch, a gym teacher at Bessie Coleman School, records the number of sit-ups each student can do. Nila used her data to make a graph showing the number of sit-ups she could do each year.

   A. Describe the graph.
   B. If you read the graph from left to right, do the points go uphill or downhill?
   C. What does the graph tell you about the number of sit-ups Nila can do?
   D. Do the points lie close to a straight line? If so, use a ruler to draw a best-fit line.
   E. If possible, predict the number of sit-ups Nila will be able to do when she is 12.
   F. Does knowing Nila's age help you predict the number of sit-ups she can do?

Nila's Sit-Ups

Number of Sit-Ups vs. Age in Years

Unit Resource Guide - page 126

Unit Resource Guide (p. 126)

Using Best-Fit Lines

1. **A.** Answers will vary. Students may state that the points tend to go uphill or that Nila can do more and more sit-ups as she gets older.*

   B. uphill

   C. Answers will vary. Nila can do more and more sit-ups as she gets older. She made no progress in the number of sit-ups she could do between the ages of 8 and 9.

   D. Yes

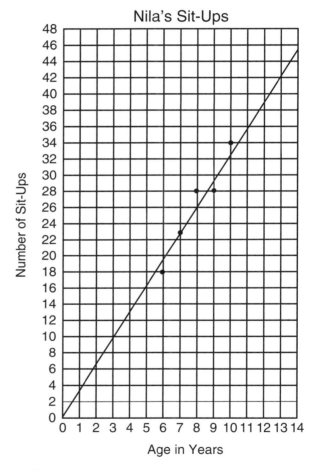

Nila's Sit-Ups

   E. Predictions will vary. About 39 or 40. Accept predictions between 37 and 42 sit-ups.

   F. Yes

*Answers and/or discussion are included in the Lesson Guide.

Unit Resource Guide (pp. 127–128)

2. **A.** Answers will vary. Students might say that John is becoming a faster runner or that the graph tends to go downhill.

B. downhill

C. Yes

John's Times for Running a Mile

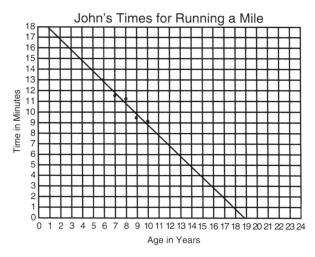

D. Predictions will vary. About 7 minutes.

E. Predictions will vary. According to our graph, John will run the mile in one minute. This is impossible. Students should see that extrapolating this far beyond the last data point is unreliable.*

F. Yes, but not for values far beyond the data points.*

3.* **A.** Descriptions will vary. The points on the graph are scattered in no apparent order.

B. No

C. No

D. Students should see that they cannot make reliable predictions on the graph since there is no pattern.

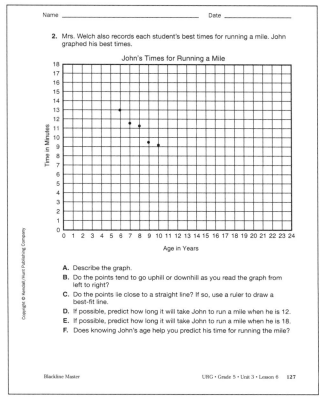

Name _____ Date _____

2. Mrs. Welch also records each student's best times for running a mile. John graphed his best times.

John's Times for Running a Mile

A. Describe the graph.
B. Do the points tend to go uphill or downhill as you read the graph from left to right?
C. Do the points lie close to a straight line? If so, use a ruler to draw a best-fit line.
D. If possible, predict how long it will take John to run a mile when he is 12.
E. If possible, predict how long it will take John to run a mile when he is 18.
F. Does knowing John's age help you predict his time for running the mile?

Blackline Master   URG • Grade 5 • Unit 3 • Lesson 6   **127**

Unit Resource Guide - page 127

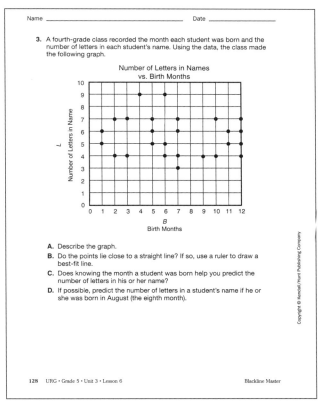

Name _____ Date _____

3. A fourth-grade class recorded the month each student was born and the number of letters in each student's name. Using the data, the class made the following graph.

Number of Letters in Names vs. Birth Months

A. Describe the graph.
B. Do the points lie close to a straight line? If so, use a ruler to draw a best-fit line.
C. Does knowing the month a student was born help you predict the number of letters in his or her name?
D. If possible, predict the number of letters in a student's name if he or she was born in August (the eighth month).

128   URG • Grade 5 • Unit 3 • Lesson 6   Blackline Master

Unit Resource Guide - page 128

*Answers and/or discussion are included in the Lesson Guide.

URG • Grade 5 • Unit 3 • Lesson 6 • Answer Key   **137**

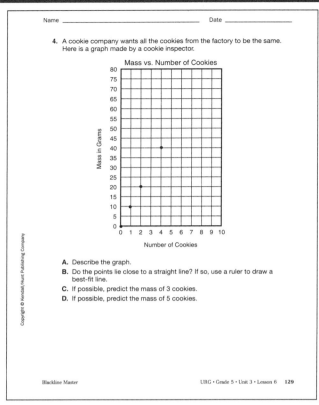

Unit Resource Guide - page 129

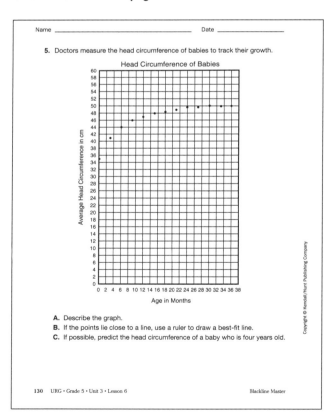

Unit Resource Guide - page 130

*Answers and/or discussion are included in the Lesson Guide.

Unit Resource Guide (pp. 129–130)

4. **A.** Descriptions will vary. The points on the graph go uphill and the more cookies you have, the more mass there is.

   B. Yes, the points lie on a straight line.

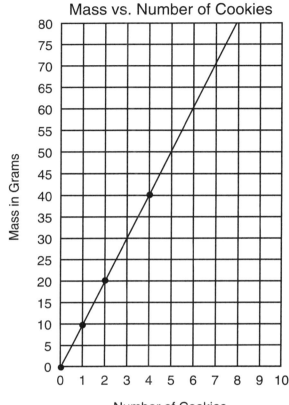

   C. 30 grams
   D. 50 grams

5. **A.** Descriptions will vary. The points tend to go uphill, but not in a line. They go uphill in a curve and level off.

   B. The points lie on a curve, so it does not make sense to draw a best-fit line.*

   C. Predictions will vary. About 42 cm. Accept predictions between 41 and 43 cm.*

Unit Resource Guide (p. 131)

6. A. Descriptions will vary. The points tend to go downhill and as the years go by, women are becoming faster swimmers.

B.

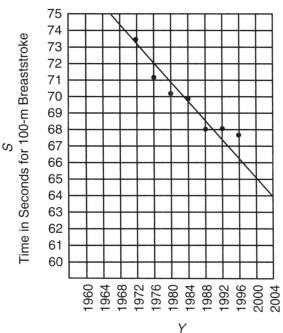

Winning Times for the Women's Olympic Breaststroke

7. The Mass vs. Number of Cookies graph. Its points lie on a straight line.

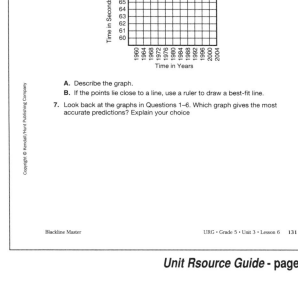

Unit Rsource Guide - page 131

Optional Lesson 7

Speedy Problems

Lesson Overview

Students solve a variety of multistep word problems. They make choices about the tools they use to solve the problems.

Key Content

- Solving multistep word problems.
- Communicating solutions orally and in writing.
- Choosing appropriate methods and tools to calculate (calculator, pencil and paper, or mental math).
- Choosing to find an estimate or an exact answer.

Homework

Assign some or all of the problems for homework.

Assessment

Assess students' work on *Question 6.*

Materials List

Supplies and Copies

Student	Teacher
Supplies for Each Student • calculator	**Supplies**
Copies	**Copies/Transparencies**

All blackline masters including assessment, transparency, and DPP masters are also on the Teacher Resource CD.

Student Books

Speedy Problems (*Student Guide* Page 99)
Student Rubric: *Telling* (*Student Guide* Appendix C and Inside Back Cover)

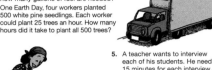

Speedy Problems

Use appropriate tools to solve the following problems.

1. A salesperson has to drive 500 miles. For the first three hours, she drove at 65 miles per hour. For the next two hours, she drove at 55 miles per hour. How many more miles does she have left to drive?

2. John bicycles for 2 hours at a speed of 15 miles per hour. How many hours will it take Shannon to cover the same distance at a speed of 10 miles per hour?

3. A truck driver drives 1000 miles. The truck uses a gallon of diesel fuel for every 15 miles. About how many gallons of fuel are needed?

4. One Earth Day, four workers planted 500 white pine seedlings. Each worker could plant 25 trees an hour. How many hours did it take to plant all 500 trees?

5. A teacher wants to interview each of his students. He needs 15 minutes for each interview. How long, in hours and minutes, will it take him to interview all 25 students in his class?

6. Alexis, Ana, and Felicia each ate fractions of pie for dessert. Alexis ate $\frac{2}{5}$ of a pie. Ana ate $\frac{2}{3}$ of a pie. Felicia ate $\frac{1}{4}$ of a pie.

   A. If all the pies were the same size, who ate the most pie? Explain.

   B. Who ate the least pie? Tell how you know.

7. Lin, Manny, and Arti each bought the same size box of pencils. One month later, $\frac{3}{4}$ of Lin's pencils are missing; $\frac{1}{8}$ of Manny's pencils are missing; $\frac{6}{8}$ of Arti's pencils are missing.

   A. Who lost the most pencils?

   B. Who lost the least number of pencils?

Student Guide - page 99 (Answers on p. 143)

This problem set can serve several purposes. It allows students to practice choosing appropriate methods for solving problems. It also provides practice with a variety of problem types and math concepts. Common and useful strategies students can use to solve the problems include: table building, guessing and checking, drawing pictures, looking for an easier related problem, estimating, and working backwards. Students may choose to use paper and pencil, mental math, or calculators to compute. For some problems an exact answer is necessary. For others, an estimate is appropriate.

Homework and Practice

Assign some or all of the problems for homework.

Assessment

Ask students to write their solutions to **Question 6.** Encourage them to use the Student Rubric: *Telling* to guide their work. (The Student Rubrics are on the inside back cover of the *Student Guide*. The Student Rubric: *Telling* is also in Appendix A of the *Student Guide*.) Use the Telling dimension of the *TIMS Multidimensional Rubric* in the Assessment section of the *Teacher Implementation Guide* to score students' work.

At a Glance

Teaching the Activity

1. Students solve *Questions 1–7* on the *Speedy Problems* Activity Page in the *Student Guide.* They can work individually or in small groups. Calculators should be available.
2. Students discuss their solution strategies with the class.

Homework

Assign some or all of the problems for homework.

Assessment

Assess students' work on *Question 6.*

Notes:

Answer Key • Lesson 7: Speedy Problems

Student Guide (p. 99)

Speedy Problems

1. 195 miles

2. 3 hours

3. Using mental math: $1000 \div 10 = 100$ and $1000 \div 20 = 50$, so $1000 \div 15$ is about 75 gallons. Using a calculator $1000 \div 15 = 66.666667$ or about 67 gallons.

4. 5 hours

5. 6 hours and 15 minutes

6. **A.** Ana ate $\frac{2}{3}$ of the pie which is the most. Possible strategy using benchmarks: $\frac{1}{6}$ and $\frac{2}{5}$ are less than $\frac{1}{2}$ since the numerators are less than half the denominators; $\frac{2}{3}$ is greater than $\frac{1}{2}$ since the numerator is more than half the denominator. So, $\frac{2}{3}$ is the largest fraction.

   B. Felicia ate $\frac{1}{6}$ of a pie which is the least; $\frac{1}{6}$ is the smallest fraction since it is close to zero, $\frac{2}{5}$ is close to $\frac{1}{2}$, and $\frac{2}{3}$ is greater than $\frac{1}{2}$.

7. **A.** Arti lost the most pencils.

   B. Manny lost the least number of pencils.

Speedy Problems

Use appropriate tools to solve the following problems.

1. A salesperson has to drive 500 miles. For the first three hours, she drove at 65 miles per hour. For the next two hours, she drove at 55 miles per hour. How many more miles does she have left to drive?

2. John bicycles for 2 hours at a speed of 15 miles per hour. How many hours will it take Shannon to cover the same distance at a speed of 10 miles per hour?

3. A truck driver drives 1000 miles. The truck uses a gallon of diesel fuel for every 15 miles. About how many gallons of fuel are needed?

4. One Earth Day, four workers planted 500 white pine seedlings. Each worker could plant 25 trees an hour. How many hours did it take to plant all 500 trees?

5. A teacher wants to interview each of his students. He needs 15 minutes for each interview. How long, in hours and minutes, will it take him to interview all 25 students in his class?

6. Alexis, Ana, and Felicia each ate fractions of pie for dessert. Alexis ate $\frac{2}{5}$ of a pie. Ana ate $\frac{2}{3}$ of a pie. Felicia ate $\frac{1}{6}$ of a pie.

   A. If all the pies were the same size, who ate the most pie? Explain.

   B. Who ate the least pie? Tell how you know.

7. Lin, Manny, and Arti each bought the same size box of pencils. One month later, $\frac{2}{3}$ of Lin's pencils are missing; $\frac{1}{6}$ of Manny's pencils are missing; $\frac{5}{8}$ of Arti's pencils are missing.

   A. Who lost the most pencils?

   B. Who lost the least number of pencils?

Speedy Problems   SG • Grade 5 • Unit 3 • Lesson 7   **99**

Student Guide - page 99

Name _____ Date _____

Unit 3 Home Practice

PART 1 *Triangle Flash Cards: 2s and 3s*

Study for the quiz on the multiplication and division facts for the 2s and 3s. Take home your *Triangle Flash Cards: 2s and 3s* and your list of facts you need to study.

Ask a family member to choose one flash card at a time. To quiz you on a multiplication fact, he or she should cover the corner containing the highest number. Multiply the two uncovered numbers.

To quiz you on a division fact, your partner can cover one of the smaller numbers. One of the smaller numbers on each card is circled. The other has a square around it. Use the two uncovered numbers to solve a division fact.

Now mix up the multiplication and division facts. Your partner should sometimes cover the highest number, sometimes cover the circled number, and sometimes cover the number in the square.

Your teacher will tell you when the quiz on the 2s and 3s will be given.

PART 2 **Rounding Numbers**

Drawing number lines (or just thinking of number lines) may help you with Questions 1 and 2.

1. Round the following numbers to the nearest hundred.
   A. 213   B. 589   C. 88

   D. 1486   E. 2815   F. 5987

2. Round the following to the nearest thousand.
   A. 1286   B. 2815   C. 5987

   D. 1099   E. 1909   F. 21,643

FRACTIONS AND RATIOS   DAB • Grade 5 • Unit 3   **27**

Discovery Assignment Book - page 27

Name _____ Date _____

PART 3 **Fractions**

1. Name a fraction between $\frac{1}{6}$ and 1. _____
2. Name a fraction between $\frac{1}{3}$ and 1. _____
3. Name a fraction with a denominator of 4 that is between 0 and 1. _____
4. Name a fraction greater than $\frac{1}{2}$ with a denominator of 8. _____
5. Name a fraction between $\frac{6}{8}$ and 1. _____
6. Which is greater:
   A. $\frac{1}{10}$ or $\frac{1}{12}$? _____
   B. $\frac{5}{8}$ or $\frac{3}{8}$? _____
   C. $\frac{7}{6}$ or 1? _____
   D. $\frac{1}{2}$ or $\frac{8}{10}$? _____

PART 4 **Number Operations**

1. Use paper and pencil to solve the following problems. Show your work on a separate sheet of paper. Estimate to make sure your answers are reasonable.
   A. $18 \times 36 =$ _____   B. $7430 + 578 =$ _____
   C. $8032 - 725 =$ _____   D. $623 \times 7 =$ _____
   E. $3419 + 7834 =$ _____   F. $2950 \times 5 =$ _____

2. Find the amount of change each person will receive in the following problems. For each, name the least number of coins and bills. Estimate to make sure your answers are reasonable.
   A. Manny buys a hamburger for $3.99, a baked potato for $1.79, and a drink for $1.29. He gives the salesclerk a $10 bill. How much change will he receive?

   B. Lin buys 3 gallons of bubble bath at $3.39 each. If Lin gives the salesclerk a $20 bill, how much change will she receive?

28   DAB • Grade 5 • Unit 3   FRACTIONS AND RATIOS

Discovery Assignment Book - page 28

Discovery Assignment Book (p. 27)

Part 2. Rounding Numbers

1. A. 200
   B. 600
   C. 100
   D. 1500
   E. 2800
   F. 6000

2. A. 1000
   B. 3000
   C. 6000
   D. 1000
   E. 2000
   F. 22,000

Discovery Assignment Book (p. 28)

Part 3. Fractions

1. Answers will vary. One possible solution is $\frac{2}{6}$.
2. Answers will vary. One possible solution is $\frac{2}{3}$.
3. Answers will vary. One possible solution is $\frac{1}{4}$.
4. Answers will vary. One possible solution is $\frac{5}{8}$.
5. Answers will vary. One possible solution is $\frac{7}{8}$.
6. A. $\frac{1}{10}$ B. $\frac{5}{8}$
   C. $\frac{7}{6}$ D. $\frac{8}{10}$

Part 4. Number Operations

1. A. 648   B. 8008
   C. 7307   D. 4361
   E. 11,253   F. 14,750

2. A. $2.93; 2 dollars, 3 quarters, 1 dime, 1 nickel, 3 pennies
   B. $9.83; 9 dollars, 3 quarters, 1 nickel, 3 pennies

Discovery Assignment Book (p. 29)

Part 5. Exercising at the Gym

1.–2.

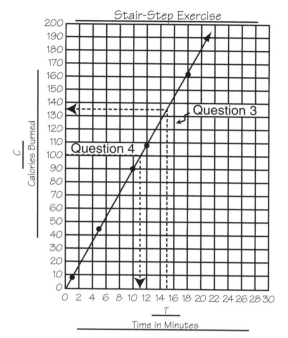

3. About 135 calories. Answers will vary slightly. Students can show their work on the graph.

4. About 11 minutes. Answers will vary. Students can show their work for this problem on the graph.

5. **A.** Answers will vary. One possible ratio is
   $\frac{90 \text{ calories}}{10 \text{ minutes}}$.

   B. Answers will vary depending on ratio given in 5A. Possible solutions for sample ratio include $\frac{180 \text{ calories}}{20 \text{ minutes}}$ and $\frac{270 \text{ calories}}{30 \text{ minutes}}$.

   C. Answers will vary. One possible solution using the answer to **Question 3** is
   $\frac{90 \text{ calories} \times 3}{10 \text{ minutes} \times 3} = \frac{270 \text{ calories}}{30 \text{ minutes}}$.

Name _____ Date _____

PART 5 Exercising at the Gym
You will need a piece of graph paper to complete this part.

Irma's mother exercises on a stair-step machine for 18 minutes. She exercises at the same rate for the entire time. The following data table shows how many calories she burned at various times.

Time T	Calories Burned C
1	9
5	45
10	90
12	108
18	162

1. Make a point graph of the data on a piece of graph paper. Graph time on the horizontal axis. Be sure to label the axes and to give your graph a title.

2. Use a ruler to fit a line to the points.

3. About how many calories did Irma's mother burn after 15 minutes? How did you decide?

4. About how long did it take her to burn 100 calories? How did you decide?

5. A. Choose a point on the graph and use it to write a ratio of calories burned to time taken. (Be sure to include units.)

   B. Write two more ratios equal to the ratio in Question 5A.

   C. If Irma's mother exercised at the same rate for 30 minutes on the stair-step machine, how many calories would she burn? Explain your solution.

Discovery Assignment Book - page 29

Discovery Assignment Book (p. 30)

PART 6 A Fraction More

1. Complete the following number sentences. The Number Lines for Fractohoppers chart you completed in Lesson 3 or the chart in Lesson 4 of the *Student Guide* may help you solve some of the problems.

   A. $\frac{1}{3} = \frac{2}{n}$ B. $\frac{9}{12} = \frac{n}{4}$ C. $\frac{2}{6} = \frac{n}{12}$

   D. $\frac{5}{8} = \frac{15}{n}$ E. $\frac{20}{70} = \frac{n}{7}$ F. $\frac{7}{9} = \frac{n}{36}$

   G. $\frac{3}{5} = \frac{n}{25}$ H. $\frac{4}{40} = \frac{1}{n}$ I. $\frac{2}{3} = \frac{8}{n}$

2. Write each mixed number as an improper fraction.

   A. $1\frac{1}{4}$ B. $5\frac{2}{3}$ C. $2\frac{7}{8}$ D. $3\frac{3}{5}$

3. Write each improper fraction as a mixed number.

   A. $\frac{9}{4}$ B. $\frac{20}{6}$ C. $\frac{21}{2}$ D. $\frac{23}{12}$

4. Put each of the following sets of fractions in order from smallest to largest.

   A. $\frac{9}{5}, \frac{9}{10}, \frac{9}{2}, \frac{9}{12}$ B. $\frac{5}{6}, \frac{8}{7}, \frac{7}{12}, \frac{1}{8}$

   C. $\frac{6}{6}, \frac{3}{6}, \frac{10}{6}, \frac{2}{6}$ D. $\frac{3}{20}, \frac{3}{2}, \frac{9}{11}, \frac{9}{16}$

Discovery Assignment Book - page 30

Part 6. A Fraction More

1. A. $\frac{1}{3} = \frac{2}{6}$

   B. $\frac{9}{12} = \frac{3}{4}$

   C. $\frac{2}{6} = \frac{4}{12}$

   D. $\frac{5}{8} = \frac{15}{24}$

   E. $\frac{20}{70} = \frac{2}{7}$

   F. $\frac{7}{9} = \frac{28}{36}$

   G. $\frac{3}{5} = \frac{15}{25}$

   H. $\frac{4}{40} = \frac{1}{10}$

   I. $\frac{2}{3} = \frac{8}{12}$

2. A. $\frac{5}{4}$

   B. $\frac{17}{3}$

   C. $\frac{23}{8}$

   D. $\frac{18}{5}$

3. A. $2\frac{1}{4}$

   B. $3\frac{2}{6}$ or $3\frac{1}{3}$

   C. $10\frac{1}{2}$

   D. $1\frac{11}{12}$

4. A. $\frac{9}{12}, \frac{9}{10}, \frac{9}{5}, \frac{9}{2}$

   B. $\frac{1}{8}, \frac{7}{12}, \frac{5}{6}, \frac{8}{7}$

   C. $\frac{2}{6}, \frac{3}{6}, \frac{6}{6}, \frac{10}{6}$

   D. $\frac{3}{20}, \frac{9}{16}, \frac{9}{11}, \frac{3}{2}$

Glossary

This glossary provides definitions of key vocabulary terms in the Grade 5 lessons. Locations of key vocabulary terms in the curriculum are included with each definition. Components Key: URG = *Unit Resource Guide* and SG = *Student Guide.*

A

Acute Angle (URG Unit 6; SG Unit 6)
An angle that measures less than 90º.

Acute Triangle (URG Unit 6 & Unit 15; SG Unit 6 & Unit 15)
A triangle that has only acute angles.

All-Partials Multiplication Method (URG Unit 2)
A paper-and-pencil method for solving multiplication problems. Each partial product is recorded on a separate line. (*See also* partial product.)

$$\begin{array}{r} 186 \\ \times\ 3 \\ \hline 18 \\ 240 \\ 300 \\ \hline 558 \end{array}$$

Altitude of a Triangle (URG Unit 15; SG Unit 15)
A line segment from a vertex of a triangle perpendicular to the opposite side or to the line extending the opposite side; also, the length of this line. The altitude is also called the height of the triangle.

Angle (URG Unit 6; SG Unit 6)
The amount of turning or the amount of opening between two rays that have the same endpoint.

Arc (URG Unit 14; SG Unit 14)
Part of a circle between two points. (*See also* circle.)

Area (URG Unit 4 & Unit 15; SG Unit 4 & Unit 15)
A measurement of size. The area of a shape is the amount of space it covers, measured in square units.

Average (URG Unit 1 & Unit 4; SG Unit 1 & Unit 4)
A number that can be used to represent a typical value in a set of data. (*See also* mean, median, and mode.)

Axes (URG Unit 10; SG Unit 10)
Reference lines on a graph. In the Cartesian coordinate system, the axes are two perpendicular lines that meet at the origin. The singular of axes is axis.

B

Base of a Triangle (URG Unit 15; SG Unit 15)
One of the sides of a triangle; also, the length of the side. A perpendicular line drawn from the vertex opposite the base is called the height or altitude of the triangle.

Base of an Exponent (URG Unit 2; SG Unit 2)
When exponents are used, the number being multiplied. In $3^4 = 3 \times 3 \times 3 \times 3 = 81$, the 3 is the base and the 4 is the exponent. The 3 is multiplied by itself 4 times.

Base-Ten Pieces (URG Unit 2; SG Unit 2)
A set of manipulatives used to model our number system as shown in the figure below. Note that a skinny is made of 10 bits, a flat is made of 100 bits, and a pack is made of 1000 bits.

Base-Ten Shorthand (URG Unit 2)
A graphical representation of the base-ten pieces as shown below.

Nickname	Picture	Shorthand
bit	▱	•
skinny	▭	/
flat	▱	▱
pack	▱	▱

Benchmarks (SG Unit 7)
Numbers convenient for comparing and ordering numbers, e.g., $0, \frac{1}{2}, 1$ are convenient benchmarks for comparing and ordering fractions.

Best-Fit Line (URG Unit 3; SG Unit 3)
The line that comes closest to the points on a point graph.

Binning Data (URG Unit 8; SG Unit 8)
Placing data from a data set with a large number of values or large range into intervals in order to more easily see patterns in the data.

Bit (URG Unit 2; SG Unit 2)
A cube that measures 1 cm on each edge.
It is the smallest of the base-ten pieces and is often used to represent 1. (*See also* base-ten pieces.)

C

Cartesian Coordinate System (URG Unit 10; SG Unit 10)
A method of locating points on a flat surface by means of an ordered pair of numbers. This method is named after its originator, René Descartes. (*See also* coordinates.)

Categorical Variable (URG Unit 1; SG Unit 1)
Variables with values that are not numbers. (*See also* variable and value.)

Center of a Circle (URG Unit 14; SG Unit 14)
The point such that every point on a circle is the same distance from it. (*See also* circle.)

Centiwheel (URG Unit 7; SG Unit 7)
A circle divided into 100 equal sections used in exploring fractions, decimals, and percents.

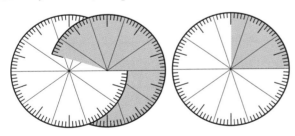

Central Angle (URG Unit 14; SG Unit 14)
An angle whose vertex is at the center of a circle.

Certain Event (URG Unit 7; SG Unit 7)
An event that has a probability of 1 (100%).

Chord (URG Unit 14; SG Unit 14)
A line segment that connects two points on a circle. (*See also* circle.)

Circle (URG Unit 14; SG Unit 14)
A curve that is made up of all the points that are the same distance from one point, the center.

Circumference (URG Unit 14; SG Unit 14)
The distance around a circle.

Common Denominator (URG Unit 5 & Unit 11; SG Unit 5 & Unit 11)
A denominator that is shared by two or more fractions. A common denominator is a common multiple of the denominators of the fractions. 15 is a common denominator of $\frac{2}{3} (= \frac{10}{15})$ and $\frac{4}{5} (= \frac{12}{15})$ since 15 is divisible by both 3 and 5.

Common Fraction (URG Unit 7; SG Unit 7)
Any fraction that is written with a numerator and denominator that are whole numbers. For example, $\frac{3}{4}$ and $\frac{9}{4}$ are both common fractions. (*See also* decimal fraction.)

Commutative Property of Addition (URG Unit 2)
The order of the addends in an addition problem does not matter, e.g., $7 + 3 = 3 + 7$.

Commutative Property of Multiplication (URG Unit 2)
The order of the factors in a multiplication problem does not matter, e.g., $7 \times 3 = 3 \times 7$. (*See also* turn-around facts.)

Compact Method (URG Unit 2)
Another name for what is considered the traditional multiplication algorithm.

$$\begin{array}{r} {}^{2}{}^{1}186 \\ \times\ 3 \\ \hline 558 \end{array}$$

Composite Number (URG Unit 11; SG Unit 11)
A number that has more than two distinct factors. For example, 9 has three factors (1, 3, 9) so it is a composite number.

Concentric Circles (URG Unit 14; SG Unit 14)
Circles that have the same center.

Congruent (URG Unit 6 & Unit 10; SG Unit 6)
Figures that are the same shape and size. Polygons are congruent when corresponding sides have the same length and corresponding angles have the same measure.

Conjecture (URG Unit 11; SG Unit 11)
A statement that has not been proved to be true, nor shown to be false.

Convenient Number (URG Unit 2; SG Unit 2)
A number used in computation that is close enough to give a good estimate, but is also easy to compute with mentally, e.g., 25 and 30 are convenient numbers for 27.

Convex (URG Unit 6)
A shape is convex if for any two points in the shape, the line segment between the points is also inside the shape.

Coordinates (URG Unit 10; SG Unit 10)
An ordered pair of numbers that locates points on a flat surface relative to a pair of coordinate axes. For example, in the ordered pair (4, 5), the first number (coordinate) is the distance from the point to the vertical axis and the second coordinate is the distance from the point to the horizontal axis. (*See also* axes.)

Corresponding Parts (URG Unit 10; SG Unit 10)
Matching parts in two or more figures. In the figure
below, Sides AB and A'B' are corresponding parts.

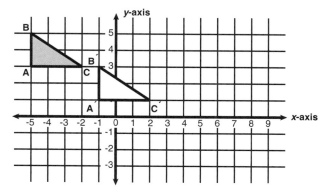

Cryptography (SG Unit 11) The study of secret codes.

Cubic Centimeter (URG Unit 13)
The volume of a cube that is one centimeter long on
each edge.

D

Data (SG Unit 1)
Information collected in an experiment or survey.

Decagon (URG Unit 6; SG Unit 6)
A ten-sided, ten-angled polygon.

Decimal (URG Unit 7; SG Unit 7)
1. A number written using the base ten place value
   system.
2. A number containing a decimal point.

Decimal Fraction (URG Unit 7; SG Unit 7)
A fraction written as a decimal. For example, 0.75 and
0.4 are decimal fractions and $\frac{75}{100}$ and $\frac{4}{10}$ are the equivalent
common fractions.

Degree (URG Unit 6; SG Unit 6)
A degree (°) is a unit of measure for angles. There are
360 degrees in a circle.

Denominator (URG Unit 3; SG Unit 3)
The number below the line in a fraction. The denominator indicates the number of equal parts in which the unit
whole is divided. For example, the 5 is the denominator
in the fraction $\frac{2}{5}$. In this case the unit whole is divided into
five equal parts. (*See also* numerator.)

Density (URG Unit 13; SG Unit 13)
The ratio of an object's mass to its volume.

Diagonal (URG Unit 6)
A line segment that connects nonadjacent corners of
a polygon.

Diameter (URG Unit 14; SG Unit 14)
1. A line segment that connects two points on a circle
   and passes through the center.
2. The length of this line segment.

Digit (SG Unit 2)
Any one of the ten symbols 0, 1, 2, 3, 4, 5, 6, 7, 8, 9.
The number 37 is made up of the digits 3 and 7.

Dividend (URG Unit 4 & Unit 9; SG Unit 4 & Unit 9)
The number that is divided in a division problem,
e.g., 12 is the dividend in 12 ÷ 3 = 4.

Divisor (URG Unit 2, Unit 4, & Unit 9; SG Unit 2,
      Unit 4, & Unit 9)
In a division problem, the number by which another
number is divided. In the problem 12 ÷ 4 = 3, the 4
is the divisor, the 12 is the dividend, and the 3 is the
quotient.

Dodecagon (URG Unit 6; SG Unit 6)
A twelve-sided, twelve-angled polygon.

E

Endpoint (URG Unit 6; SG Unit 6)
The point at either end of a line segment or the point at
the end of a ray.

Equally Likely (URG Unit 7; SG Unit 7)
When events have the same probability, they are called
equally likely.

Equidistant (URG Unit 14)
At the same distance.

Equilateral Triangle (URG Unit 6, Unit 14, & Unit 15)
A triangle that has all three sides equal in length. An
equilateral triangle also has three equal angles.

Equivalent Fractions (URG Unit 3; SG Unit 3)
Fractions that have the same value, e.g., $\frac{2}{4} = \frac{1}{2}$.

Estimate (URG Unit 2; SG Unit 2)
1. To find *about* how many (as a verb).
2. A number that is *close to* the desired number (as a
   noun).

Expanded Form (SG Unit 2)
A way to write numbers that shows the place value of
each digit, e.g., 4357 = 4000 + 300 + 50 + 7.

Exponent (URG Unit 2 & Unit 11; SG Unit 2 & Unit 11)
The number of times the base is multiplied by itself.
In $3^4 = 3 \times 3 \times 3 \times 3 = 81$, the 3 is the base and the
4 is the exponent. The 3 is multiplied by itself 4 times.

Extrapolation (URG Unit 13; SG Unit 13)
Using patterns in data to make predictions or to estimate
values that lie beyond the range of values in the set of
data.

F

Fact Families (URG Unit 2; SG Unit 2)
Related math facts, e.g., 3 × 4 = 12, 4 × 3 = 12,
12 ÷ 3 = 4, 12 ÷ 4 = 3.

Factor Tree (URG Unit 11; SG Unit 11)
A diagram that shows the prime factorization of a number.

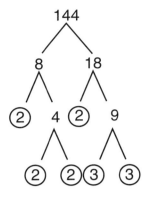

Factors (URG Unit 2 & Unit 11; SG Unit 2 & Unit 11)
1. In a multiplication problem, the numbers that are multiplied together. In the problem $3 \times 4 = 12$, 3 and 4 are the factors.
2. Numbers that divide a number evenly, e.g., 1, 2, 3, 4, 6, and 12 are all the factors of 12.

Fair Game (URG Unit 7; SG Unit 7)
A game in which it is equally likely that any player will win.

Fewest Pieces Rule (URG Unit 2)
Using the least number of base-ten pieces to represent a number. (*See also* base-ten pieces.)

Fixed Variables (URG Unit 4; SG Unit 3 & Unit 4)
Variables in an experiment that are held constant or not changed, in order to find the relationship between the manipulated and responding variables. These variables are often called controlled variables. (*See also* manipulated variable and responding variable.)

Flat (URG Unit 2; SG Unit 2)
A block that measures 1 cm $\times$ 10 cm $\times$ 10 cm. It is one of the base-ten pieces and is often used to represent 100. (*See also* base-ten pieces.)

Flip (URG Unit 10; SG Unit 10)
A motion of the plane in which the plane is reflected over a line so that any point and its image are the same distance from the line.

Forgiving Division Method
(URG Unit 4; SG Unit 4)
A paper-and-pencil method for division in which successive partial quotients are chosen and subtracted from the dividend, until the remainder is less than the divisor. The sum of the partial quotients is the quotient. For example, $644 \div 7$ can be solved as shown at the right.

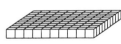

Formula (SG Unit 11 & Unit 14)
A number sentence that gives a general rule. A formula for finding the area of a rectangle is Area = length $\times$ width, or $A = l \times w$.

Fraction (URG Unit 7; SG Unit 7)
A number that can be written as a/b where a and b are whole numbers and b is not zero.

G

Googol (URG Unit 2)
A number that is written as a 1 with 100 zeroes after it (10^{100}).

Googolplex (URG Unit 2)
A number that is written as a 1 with a googol of zeroes after it.

H

Height of a Triangle (URG Unit 15; SG Unit 15)
A line segment from a vertex of a triangle perpendicular to the opposite side or to the line extending the opposite side; also, the length of this line. The height is also called the altitude.

Hexagon (URG Unit 6; SG Unit 6)
A six-sided polygon.

Hypotenuse (URG Unit 15; SG Unit 15)
The longest side of a right triangle.

I

Image (URG Unit 10; SG Unit 10)
The result of a transformation, in particular a slide (translation) or a flip (reflection), in a coordinate plane. The new figure after the slide or flip is the image of the old figure.

Impossible Event (URG Unit 7; SG Unit 7)
An event that has a probability of 0 or 0%.

Improper Fraction (URG Unit 3; SG Unit 3)
A fraction in which the numerator is greater than or equal to the denominator. An improper fraction is greater than or equal to one.

Infinite (URG Unit 2)
Never ending, immeasurably great, unlimited.

Interpolation (URG Unit 13; SG Unit 13)
Making predictions or estimating values that lie between data points in a set of data.

Intersect (URG Unit 14)
To meet or cross.

Isosceles Triangle (URG Unit 6 & Unit 15)
A triangle that has at least two sides of equal length.

J

K

L

Lattice Multiplication
(URG Unit 9; SG Unit 9)
A method for multiplying that uses a lattice to arrange the partial products so the digits are correctly placed in the correct place value columns. A lattice for $43 \times 96 = 4128$ is shown at the right.

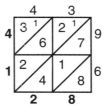

Legs of a Right Triangle (URG Unit 15; SG Unit 15)
The two sides of a right triangle that form the right angle.

Length of a Rectangle (URG Unit 4 & Unit 15; SG Unit 4 & Unit 15)
The distance along one side of a rectangle.

Line
A set of points that form a straight path extending infinitely in two directions.

Line of Reflection (URG Unit 10)
A line that acts as a mirror so that after a shape is flipped over the line, corresponding points are at the same distance (equidistant) from the line.

Line Segment (URG Unit 14)
A part of a line between and including two points, called the endpoints.

Liter (URG Unit 13)
Metric unit used to measure volume. A liter is a little more than a quart.

Lowest Terms (SG Unit 11)
A fraction is in lowest terms if the numerator and denominator have no common factor greater than 1.

M

Manipulated Variable (URG Unit 4; SG Unit 4)
In an experiment, the variable with values known at the beginning of the experiment. The experimenter often chooses these values before data is collected. The manipulated variable is often called the independent variable.

Mass (URG Unit 13)
The amount of matter in an object.

Mean (URG Unit 1 & Unit 4; SG Unit 1 & Unit 4)
An average of a set of numbers that is found by adding the values of the data and dividing by the number of values.

Measurement Division (URG Unit 4)
Division as equal grouping. The total number of objects and the number of objects in each group are known. The number of groups is the unknown. For example, tulip bulbs come in packages of 8. If 216 bulbs are sold, how many packages are sold?

Median (URG Unit 1; SG Unit 1)
For a set with an odd number of data arranged in order, it is the middle number. For an even number of data arranged in order, it is the mean of the two middle numbers.

Meniscus (URG Unit 13)
The curved surface formed when a liquid creeps up the side of a container (for example, a graduated cylinder).

Milliliter (ml) (URG Unit 13)
A measure of capacity in the metric system that is the volume of a cube that is one centimeter long on each side.

Mixed Number (URG Unit 3; SG Unit 3)
A number that is written as a whole number followed by a fraction. It is equal to the sum of the whole number and the fraction.

Mode (URG Unit 1; SG Unit 1)
The most common value in a data set.

Mr. Origin (URG Unit 10; SG Unit 10)
A plastic figure used to represent the origin of a coordinate system and to indicate the directions of the x- and y- axes. (and possibly the z-axis).

N

N-gon (URG Unit 6; SG Unit 6)
A polygon with N sides.

Negative Number (URG Unit 10; SG Unit 10)
A number less than zero; a number to the left of zero on a horizontal number line.

Nonagon (URG Unit 6; SG Unit 6)
A nine-sided polygon.

Numerator (URG Unit 3; SG Unit 3)
The number written above the line in a fraction. For example, the 2 is the numerator in the fraction $\frac{2}{5}$. In this case, we are interested in two of the five parts. (*See also* denominator.)

Numerical Expression (URG Unit 4; SG Unit 4)
A combination of numbers and operations, e.g., $5 + 8 \div 4$.

Numerical Variable (URG Unit 1; SG Unit 1)
Variables with values that are numbers. (*See also* variable and value.)

O

Obtuse Angle (URG Unit 6; SG Unit 6)
An angle that measures more than 90°.

Obtuse Triangle (URG Unit 6 & Unit 15; SG Unit 6 & Unit 15)
A triangle that has an obtuse angle.

Octagon (URG Unit 6; SG Unit 6)
An eight-sided polygon.

Ordered Pair (URG Unit 10; SG Unit 10)
A pair of numbers that gives the coordinates of a point on a grid in relation to the origin. The horizontal coordinate is given first; the vertical coordinate is given second. For example, the ordered pair (5, 3) gives the coordinates of the point that is 5 units to the right of the origin and 3 units up.

Origin (URG Unit 10; SG Unit 10)
The point at which the *x*- and *y*-axes intersect on a coordinate plane. The origin is described by the ordered pair (0, 0) and serves as a reference point so that all the points on the plane can be located by ordered pairs.

P

Pack (URG Unit 2; SG Unit 2)
A cube that measures 10 cm on each edge. It is one of the base-ten pieces and is often used to represent 1000. (*See also* base-ten pieces.)

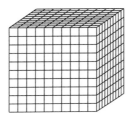

Parallel Lines
(URG Unit 6 & Unit 10)
Lines that are in the same direction. In the plane, parallel lines are lines that do not intersect.

Parallelogram (URG Unit 6)
A quadrilateral with two pairs of parallel sides.

Partial Product (URG Unit 2)
One portion of the multiplication process in the all-partials multiplication method, e.g., in the problem 3 × 186 there are three partial products: 3 × 6 = 18, 3 × 80 = 240, and 3 × 100 = 300. (*See also* all-partials multiplication method.)

Partitive Division (URG Unit 4)
Division as equal sharing. The total number of objects and the number of groups are known. The number of objects in each group is the unknown. For example, Frank has 144 marbles that he divides equally into 6 groups. How many marbles are in each group?

Pentagon (URG Unit 6; SG Unit 6)
A five-sided polygon.

Percent (URG Unit 7; SG Unit 7)
Per hundred or out of 100. A special ratio that compares a number to 100. For example, 20% (twenty percent) of the jelly beans are yellow means that out of every 100 jelly beans, 20 are yellow.

Perimeter (URG Unit 15; SG Unit 15)
The distance around a two-dimensional shape.

Period (SG Unit 2)
A group of three places in a large number, starting on the right, often separated by commas as shown at the right.

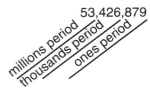

Perpendicular Lines (URG Unit 14 & Unit 15; SG Unit 14)
Lines that meet at right angles.

Pi (π) (URG Unit 14; SG Unit 14)
The ratio of the circumference to diameter of a circle. π = 3.14159265358979.... It is a nonterminating, nonrepeating decimal.

Place (SG Unit 2)
The position of a digit in a number.

Place Value (URG Unit 2; SG Unit 2)
The value of a digit in a number. For example, the 5 is in the hundreds place in 4573, so it stands for 500.

Polygon (URG Unit 6; SG Unit 6)
A two-dimensional connected figure made of line segments in which each endpoint of every side meets with an endpoint of exactly one other side.

Population (URG Unit 1 Unit 1)
A collection of persons or things whose properties will be analyzed in a survey or experiment.

Portfolio (URG Unit 2; SG Unit 2)
A collection of student work that show how a student's skills, attitudes, and knowledge change over time.

Positive Number (URG Unit 10; SG Unit 10)
A number greater than zero; a number to the right of zero on a horizontal number line.

Power (URG Unit 2; SG Unit 2)
An exponent. Read 10^4 as, "ten to the fourth power" or "ten to the fourth." We say 10,000 or 10^4 is the fourth power of ten.

Prime Factorization (URG Unit 11; SG Unit 11)
Writing a number as a product of primes. The prime factorization of 100 is 2 × 2 × 5 × 5.

Prime Number (URG Unit 11; SG Unit 11)
A number that has exactly two factors: itself and 1. For example, 7 has exactly two distinct factors, 1 and 7.

Probability (URG Unit 7; SG Unit 1 & Unit 7)
A number from 0 to 1 (0% to 100%) that describes how likely an event is to happen. The closer that the probability of an event is to one, the more likely the event will happen.

Product (URG Unit 2; SG Unit 2)
The answer to a multiplication problem. In the problem $3 \times 4 = 12$, 12 is the product.

Proper Fraction (URG Unit 3; SG Unit 3)
A fraction in which the numerator is less than the denominator. Proper fractions are less than one.

Proportion (URG Unit 3 & Unit 13; SG Unit 13)
A statement that two ratios are equal.

Protractor (URG Unit 6; SG Unit 6)
A tool for measuring angles.

Q

Quadrants (URG Unit 10; SG Unit 10)
The four sections of a coordinate grid that are separated by the axes.

Quadrilateral (URG Unit 6; SG Unit 6)
A polygon with four sides. (*See also* polygon.)

Quotient (URG Unit 4 & Unit 9; SG Unit 2, Unit 4, & Unit 9)
The answer to a division problem. In the problem $12 \div 3 = 4$, the 4 is the quotient.

R

Radius (URG Unit 14; SG Unit 14)
1. A line segment connecting the center of a circle to any point on the circle.
2. The length of this line segment.

Ratio (URG Unit 3 & Unit 12; SG Unit 3 & Unit 13)
A way to compare two numbers or quantities using division. It is often written as a fraction.

Ray (URG Unit 6; SG Unit 6)
A part of a line with one endpoint that extends indefinitely in one direction.

Rectangle (URG Unit 6; SG Unit 6)
A quadrilateral with four right angles.

Reflection (URG Unit 10)
(*See* flip.)

Regular Polygon (URG Unit 6; SG Unit 6; DAB Unit 6)
A polygon with all sides of equal length and all angles equal.

Remainder (URG Unit 4 & Unit 9; SG Unit 4 & Unit 9)
Something that remains or is left after a division problem. The portion of the dividend that is not evenly divisible by the divisor, e.g., $16 \div 5 = 3$ with 1 as a remainder.

Repeating Decimals (SG Unit 9)
A decimal fraction with one or more digits repeating without end.

Responding Variable (URG Unit 4; SG Unit 4)
The variable whose values result from the experiment. Experimenters find the values of the responding variable by doing the experiment. The responding variable is often called the dependent variable.

Rhombus (URG Unit 6; SG Unit 6)
A quadrilateral with four equal sides.

Right Angle (URG Unit 6; SG Unit 6)
An angle that measures 90°.

Right Triangle (URG Unit 6 & Unit 15; SG Unit 6 & Unit 15)
A triangle that contains a right angle.

Rubric (URG Unit 1)
A scoring guide that can be used to guide or assess student work.

S

Sample (URG Unit 1)
A part or subset of a population.

Scalene Triangle (URG Unit 15)
A triangle that has no sides that are equal in length.

Scientific Notation (URG Unit 2; SG Unit 2)
A way of writing numbers, particularly very large or very small numbers. A number in scientific notation has two factors. The first factor is a number greater than or equal to one and less than ten. The second factor is a power of 10 written with an exponent. For example, 93,000,000 written in scientific notation is 9.3×10^7.

Septagon (URG Unit 6; SG Unit 6)
A seven-sided polygon.

Side-Angle-Side (URG Unit 6 & Unit 14)
A geometric property stating that two triangles having two corresponding sides with the included angle equal are congruent.

Side-Side-Side (URG Unit 6)
A geometric property stating that two triangles having corresponding sides equal are congruent.

Sides of an Angle (URG Unit 6; SG Unit 6)
The sides of an angle are two rays with the same endpoint. (*See also* endpoint and ray.)

Sieve of Eratosthenes (SG Unit 11)
A method for separating prime numbers from nonprime numbers developed by Eratosthenes, an Egyptian librarian, in about 240 BCE.

Similar (URG Unit 6; SG Unit 6)
Similar shapes have the same shape but not necessarily the same size.

Skinny (URG Unit 2; SG Unit 2)
A block that measures 1 cm × 1 cm × 10 cm.
It is one of the base-ten pieces
and is often used to represent 10.
(*See also* base-ten pieces.)

Slide (URG Unit 10; SG Unit 10)
Moving a geometric figure in the plane by moving every
point of the figure the same distance in the same direction. Also called translation.

Speed (URG Unit 3 & Unit 5; SG Unit 3 & Unit 5)
The ratio of distance moved to time taken, e.g.,
3 miles/1 hour or 3 mph is a speed.

Square (URG Unit 6 & Unit 14; SG Unit 6)
A quadrilateral with four equal sides and four right
angles.

Square Centimeter (URG Unit 4; SG Unit 4)
The area of a square that is 1 cm long on each side.

Square Number (URG Unit 11)
A number that is the product of a whole number multiplied by itself. For example, 25 is a square number since
$5 \times 5 = 25$. A square number can be represented by a
square array with the same number of rows as columns.
A square array for 25 has 5 rows of 5 objects in each row
or 25 total objects.

Standard Form (SG Unit 2)
The traditional way to write a number, e.g., standard
form for three hundred fifty-seven is 357. (*See also*
expanded form and word form.)

Standard Units (URG Unit 4)
Internationally or nationally agreed-upon units used in
measuring variables, e.g., centimeters and inches are
standard units used to measure length and square centimeters and square inches are used to measure area.

Straight Angle (URG Unit 6; SG Unit 6)
An angle that measures 180°.

T

Ten Percent (URG Unit 4; SG Unit 4)
10 out of every hundred or $\frac{1}{10}$.

Tessellation (URG Unit 6 & Unit 10; SG Unit 6)
A pattern made up of one or more repeated shapes that
completely covers a surface without any gaps or overlaps.

Translation
(*See* slide.)

Trapezoid (URG Unit 6)
A quadrilateral with exactly one pair of parallel sides.

Triangle (URG Unit 6; SG Unit 6)
A polygon with three sides.

Triangulating (URG Unit 6; SG Unit 6)
Partitioning a polygon into two or more nonoverlapping
triangles by drawing diagonals that do not intersect.

Turn-Around Facts (URG Unit 2)
Multiplication facts that have the same factors but in a
different order, e.g., $3 \times 4 = 12$ and $4 \times 3 = 12$.
(*See also* commutative property of multiplication.)

Twin Primes (URG Unit 11; SG Unit 11)
A pair of prime numbers whose difference is 2.
For example, 3 and 5 are twin primes.

U

Unit Ratio (URG Unit 13; SG Unit 13)
A ratio with a denominator of one.

V

Value (URG Unit 1; SG Unit 1)
The possible outcomes of a variable. For example, red,
green, and blue are possible values for the variable *color*.
Two meters and 1.65 meters are possible values for the
variable *length*.

Variable (URG Unit 1; SG Unit 1)
1. An attribute or quantity that changes or varies.
   (*See also* categorical variable and numerical variable.)
2. A symbol that can stand for a variable.

Variables in Proportion (URG Unit 13; SG Unit 13)
When the ratio of two variables in an experiment is
always the same, the variables are in proportion.

Velocity (URG Unit 5; SG Unit 5)
Speed in a given direction. Speed is the ratio of the distance traveled to time taken.

Vertex (URG Unit 6; SG Unit 6)
A common point of two rays or line segments that form
an angle.

Volume (URG Unit 13)
The measure of the amount of space occupied by an
object.

W

Whole Number
Any of the numbers 0, 1, 2, 3, 4, 5, 6 and so on.

Width of a Rectangle (URG Unit 4 & Unit 15;
   SG Unit 4 & Unit 15)
The distance along one side of a rectangle is the length
and the distance along an adjacent side is the width.

Word Form (SG Unit 2)
A number expressed in words, e.g., the word form for
123 is "one hundred twenty-three." (*See also* expanded
form and standard form.)

X

Y

Z